MW01286745

Praise for *The Miracle Book*

"Noted spiritual author Anthony DeStefano helps us understand the nature of miracles, how to recognize them, and how to ask God for one. DeStefano's easy-to-read, but deeply profound, insights can help all those who are looking to our Heavenly Father and seeking His answer to their prayers."

—Timothy Cardinal Dolan, Archbishop of New York

"You might say that there is nothing more important than miracles. I certainly do. They are at the very heart of how we see God interacting with us. So this book about miracles is vitally important, and I recommend it strongly. May God use it in your life!"

—Eric Metaxas, Host, *Socrates in the City*; Author, *Bonhoeffer: Pastor, Martyr, Prophet, Spy* and *Miracles: What They Are, Why They Happen, and How They Can Change Your Life*

"Every heart wants a miracle. Every soul craves miracles' healing powers. What Anthony DeStefano offers in this book is a deeply intriguing discourse on the true nature of miracles. Are they a realignment of the natural order? Or are they a restoration of God's intended creation? Read and discover."

—Lauren Green, Chief Religion Correspondent, Fox News; Author, *Lighthouse Faith* and *Light for Today*

"Attention, miracle seekers! Are you ready to unleash the awesome power of prayer and transform your life? Anthony DeStefano's *The Miracle Book* is your personal hotline to miracles. This isn't some wishy-washy, feel-good fluff. It's a no-nonsense, step-by-step battle plan for getting answers to prayer. Your health's in trouble? Your bank account's on life support? Your emotions are a category-5 hurricane? It doesn't matter. This book's got you covered. DeStefano gives you the inside track on how to pray for God's will to be done on earth as it is in Heaven. But here's the kicker: This isn't just about getting what you want. It's about finding that soul-deep peace that makes you bulletproof against life's curveballs. So, what are you waiting for? Grab *The Miracle Book* now and start calling on God's help. Your new life is waiting on the other end of your prayer."

—**Gordon Robertson, President and CEO, Christian Broadcasting Network (CBN); Chancellor, Regent University**

"DeStefano strips away superstition and wishful thinking to present a clear-eyed, compelling case for how prayer can unlock the miraculous. A rare blend of spiritual wisdom and practical guidance."

—**Doug Keck, President and COO, Eternal Word Television Network (EWTN)**

"Anthony DeStefano's persuasively and expertly written book shows us how to bring miracles into our lives. To best 'know, love, and serve God,' we must first connect to the largest miracles of creation and life and become an essential part of a network of others who engage in regular prayer. Perhaps most importantly, we should not wait until we are desperate or terribly ill to seek out the miracles to save us but should build that connection with God beforehand. DeStefano is our powerful and articulate guide on how to bring God into our lives. In this way, prayer becomes part of our cycles of healing and health."

— **Marc Siegel, M.D., Senior Medical Analyst, Fox News**

"Without guaranteeing the impossible, Anthony DeStefano, in his one-of-a-kind *Miracle Book*, boldly attempts to answer the age-old, universal question: How can I obtain a miracle? In a calm, clear presentation, he offers those who are in desperate need of divine intervention a path forward and the best possible way to present their request before God."

— **Michael O'Neill, Host, *The Miracle Hunter***

"Anthony DeStefano cuts through the mystery of miracles with clarity, realism, and hope. *The Miracle Book* offers a no-nonsense road map to understanding how prayer intersects with the natural world. If you've ever wrestled with unanswered prayers or wondered how to align your will with God's, you'll find in this book both answers and inspiration. A powerful and practical guide to the reality of modern-day miracles."

—**Rob Wallace, Peabody Award-Winning Executive Producer and Director; Senior Producer, Barbara Walters Specials, ABC News' *20/20*, and CBS News' *60 Minutes II***

"In a world that often feels chaotic and uncertain, *The Miracle Book* is a compelling, well-reasoned take on the power of hope and persistence in the face of life's greatest trials."

—**Michael Clemente, Former Executive Producer, ABC News; Special Adviser, Trinity Broadcasting Network (TBN); Former Executive Vice President, Fox News; Former CEO, Newsmax**

"Early in *The Miracle Book*, Anthony DeStefano cuts to the chase, observing that 'there are no atheists in foxholes.' We all find ourselves in a foxhole at times in our lives, crying out for a miracle. With brilliant simplicity, Anthony lays out a practical two-way route to finding miracles—a route marked not just by seeking faith but by patiently abandoning prideful self-reliance in order to find it."

—**Doug McKelway, Former Anchor, ABC and Fox News**

The Miracle Book

Anthony DeStefano

THE MIRACLE BOOK

A Simple Guide to
Asking for the Impossible

Sophia Institute Press

Manchester, New Hampshire

Nihil Obstat: Rev. Mark Vaillancourt, Ph.D., *Censor Librorum*
***Imprimatur*: Reverend Monsignor Joseph P. LaMorte, Vicar General**
Archdiocese of New York
February 3, 2025

Sophia Institute Press
Box 5284, Manchester, NH 03108
1-800-888-9344
www.SophiaInstitute.com

Sophia Institute Press® is a registered trademark of Sophia Institute.

hardcover ISBN 978-1-64413-435-1
ebook ISBN 978-1-64413-436-8

Library of Congress Control Number: 2025936142

First printing

This book is dedicated to my beautiful wife, Jordan,
the greatest miracle God has ever given me.

*The kingdom of heaven is like treasure hidden in a field.
When a man found it, he ... sold all he had
and bought that field.*

—Matthew 13:44

*The most incredible thing about miracles
is that they happen.*

—G. K. Chesterton

Contents

1

So, You Need a Miracle?

If you're reading these words right now, you probably need a miracle.

I have no idea what kind of miracle you need. Are you facing surgery, perhaps? Have the doctors discovered a malignant tumor growing somewhere in your body? Has your mother or sister or daughter been diagnosed with a life-threatening illness?

Maybe the miracle you need is financial in nature. Maybe you can't make your mortgage payments and you're about to lose your home. Maybe you need a big break in your career or you're facing an audit or a potential scandal. Maybe you're struggling to pay your bills. Is it your job that's killing you? Is your boss about to pass you over again?

Or maybe you have serious family problems. Is your son using drugs? Is your marriage falling apart? Are you struggling with a compulsive habit or addiction? Is your drinking getting out of hand, or your eating, or your gambling? Is pornography wreaking havoc in your life? Maybe you're just lost and don't know what to do with your life. Maybe you're tired of being lonely and you desperately want to meet someone to love. Or maybe you're just unhappy and anxiety-ridden and at the end of your rope.

Whatever the problem, if you've picked up this book, I'm going to assume that you want something and that whatever it is seems out of reach and humanly impossible to obtain. I'm going to assume that you have nowhere to turn but to God. Maybe you haven't talked to Him in a long time, or maybe you pray to Him every day. Maybe you're an atheist or an agnostic, or maybe you're a devout, Bible-believing Protestant or an orthodox, churchgoing Catholic. It doesn't really matter at this moment—at least not to you. What matters is that you desire something badly. And this time it's serious. This time you mean business. This time you really need supernatural assistance, and you need it *now*. As the saying goes, "There are no atheists in foxholes." When you're under enemy fire and you feel as though you or someone you love might perish at any moment, there isn't anything you won't do or try in order to get help.

If that's where you are, I understand. Believe me, I've been there. And I've written this book to help you. Yes, I know there are many books out there on miracles—some truly great ones too. But very few of them explain in clear, concise, and theologically sound language how to pray for them. That's the purpose of this book: to be practical; to get to the nuts and bolts of the issue, despite its complexities; to assist you right this second, no matter how hopeless your situation may seem, and even if you've brought the problem on yourself.

So many people in the world are suffering, but they don't know how to go about asking God for help in a way that He will respond positively. They beg God, plead with Him, negotiate with Him, and promise Him that they'll change their ways *if only* He will grant them *this one request*. But if God fails to answer their prayer in the way they want, they lose faith in Him, or get angry at Him, or fall into despair.

There must be a better way.

This whole book really hinges on a riddle: Do miracles happen every day, or is obtaining a miracle more like winning a lottery (i.e., next to impossible)? There are three fundamental viewpoints on the question.

Some Christians think that all you need to do to obtain a miracle is to have "more faith" and to fully exercise the "authority and dominion" that was given to you by Christ, by taking advantage of the fact that you have been "baptized in the Holy Spirit."

Other fervent believers say that you can have all the faith in the world and still be refused the miracle you desire, for the simple reason that what you ask for is not in line with the will of God.

A third view—and the thesis of this book—is that there's really no riddle at all; that obtaining a miracle is both easy *and* difficult and that it involves a mysterious, divine paradox, the kind the famous Christian writer G. K. Chesterton wrote about.

One thing is for sure. No matter what our religious beliefs may be, or what degree of faith we have, we all know, deep down, that no book, no prayer, no church, no pastor, no priest, no pope, no faith healer, and no author can ever absolutely guarantee that God will grant us the specific miracle we want. After all, if we were certain to get all the miracles we asked for, they wouldn't be miracles in the first place.

The question is: Can we do *anything* to help our cause?

The 1943 film *The Song of Bernadette* contains a famous quote about miracles: "For those who believe, no explanation is necessary. For those who do not believe, no explanation is possible."[1] This book assumes that you are already a believer or that you're open to believing. As believers, we know that miracles *are* possible and that they *do* happen—and sometimes as a direct result of prayer. Not only is the anecdotal evidence for this overwhelming, but it's a biblical fact and a doctrine of faith held by practically every religion in the world. If that's the case, then is there perhaps something we can do to *increase the chances* that God will say yes to us, or at least answer us in a way that satisfies our hearts, alleviates our anxiety, and gives us true, abiding peace? That's my goal here: not to indulge in pie-in-the-sky, wishful thinking, not to engage in silly superstition, not to toy with your emotions and give you false hopes, but, rather, to provide some practical, theologically sound guidance you can put your trust in.

I grew up a skeptical New Yorker. Even though I was born and raised a Catholic, I lived as an agnostic for many years. In my youth, I wanted to be a surgeon, and most of

---

[1] This quote loosely reflects ideas from Thomas Aquinas, *Summa Theologica* (*ST*), I-II, q. 6, art. 1, trans. Fathers of the English Dominican Province (New York: Benziger Brothers, 1947).

my studies were in the sciences. Moreover, my natural disposition has always leaned more toward the carnal than the spiritual. I became committed to my Christian faith only after a long process of reading, reasoning, and investigating. It wasn't due to any mountaintop "aha" experiences.

In other words, I'm not prone to be naïve. I understand the role that emotions play in the lives of enthusiastic Christians. I understand how strong the power of suggestion can be. Most importantly, I understand the desire of some religious people to believe that every coincidence in life is the result of the direct, ordaining will of God. I understand that, and I'm sympathetic to anyone with strong spiritual convictions. But I'm simply not that kind of believer.

That admission might make you think my faith is weak. But it's not. In fact, the opposite is true. My faith has been forged in the heat of rigorous debate and steeled with a certitude born of real-life experience and suffering. I'm not quite a cynic, but I do have a highly realistic outlook on the world. My faith in God and Heaven and the ultimate victory of good over evil is profound, but I also know that our time on earth — no matter how joyful and faith-filled — will always be characterized by great sorrow and pain. That's why I'm not going to rattle off a lot of miracle stories of dubious authenticity. Those stories—many of them true and many downright silly—are available online if you want them, and they are legion. Nor will I go into eloquent raptures about the glorious spiritual visions I've been given by God—because the truth is, I haven't.

I know there aren't any magic formulas you can say that will alter God's divine plan, and sometimes the miracles we ask for so fervently are in direct contradiction to that plan. However—and this is a big however—God has given us the great privilege of freely *participating* in that plan, through our prayers and actions. Sometimes God *wants* us to ask for a miracle because He knows it's not in violation of His divine will, and He knows it will result in *His* greater glory. In fact, sometimes God will grant us a miracle only *if* we pray for it—and only if we pray for it with the right attitude and in the right spiritual state.

Which brings us back to the point of this book: I believe there are indeed things you can do to increase the likelihood of obtaining either a miracle or an extraordinary answer to prayer, and in the following pages I'm going to show you exactly what they are. I'm going to help you to do everything *in your power* to get the miracle you need. Bear in mind, I'm not guaranteeing the miracle itself—I'm guaranteeing you the *best possible chance* of getting it.

7

I must warn you that you're going to have to be actively involved in this process. This may be a simple book, but it's not an easy one. It's not a pious devotional that you can passively leaf through in your spare time. This is a practical, nuts-and-bolts handbook on one of the most serious subjects in the world. You're going to have to really think deeply and try to understand the nature of miracles, why they happen, and how they're connected to God's divine plan. More importantly, you're going to have to try to understand how your prayers and your identity as a believer can fit into that plan in such a way that they might influence the future. This is a profound mystery that has to do with the relationship between providence and free will, and between God's *ordaining* will and His *permissive* will. At its core, it has to do with your personal relationship with God.

Now, of course I don't want you to have to go through a whole book before you start the process of obtaining the miracle you want. In fact, I don't want you to waste a moment's time. No doubt you need a miracle urgently. So right here and now, I want you to begin.

Before any great undertaking, there must always be some form of preparation. Before you take the bar exam, you must study. Before you run a marathon, you must train. Before you write a book, you must do research. Before you get married, you must have a courtship. Before you buy a house, you must create a budget. Before you perform surgery, you must review your patient's history.

It's the same with obtaining a miracle. There's something you must do first. There's a way you must prepare yourself so that you can *receive* this great gift you're asking for.

What, exactly, is it?

Well, how do you receive any kind of present? The answer is, you first must extend your arms and open your hands. That's the only way you can take the present and hold it. In this case, there's a spiritual equivalent of doing just that. It involves opening yourself to God in humility. It involves letting go of your cares—if only for an instant—and extending your hands in trust. It involves saying a very basic prayer.

Think of it this way. If you need a miracle right now, you're probably full of emotions and anxieties and fears and conflicting desires and a million worries about your family and the future. Those kinds of feelings are the only "weapons" you have to defend yourself against being overwhelmed by stress and despair. It may not look like it to the people around you, but you're carrying a tremendous burden wherever you go.

But how in the world can you expect to receive God's gift of a miracle if you're already holding so much? The purpose of this preparatory prayer is to free up your hands and your mind and your heart and your soul; to make you drop your weapons and surrender to God; to be completely open and receptive.

It doesn't matter what your faith is or if you have no faith at all—you can still say this prayer. I happen to be a Catholic Christian. But you might be Evangelical or Jewish or Muslim. You might even be an atheist. At this moment, that's of no concern. This is only a first step—just a way of preparing the ground for what's to come. We'll get more into Christian theology in the next chapter. But for now, what's most important is that you humble yourself before God and admit your fundamental helplessness.

And isn't that the truth of the matter? Don't you feel weak and helpless? Isn't that why you need a miracle in the first place?

With that in mind, here's a simple prayer for you to start saying *right now*. It's something you can read silently or out loud. It's something you can say once a day or several times a day. However many times you say it, though, try to say it calmly, quietly, and without much anxiety or emotion. Picture in your mind a well-behaved, obedient, and trusting child who is asking his father for a gift. Does that child have clenched fists? Is he full of turmoil? Is he crying or pleading or throwing a tantrum? Or is the child quietly filled with anticipation and trust? For the time it takes to say this prayer, try to be like that child. Don't worry about your feelings. For just a moment, let them go. Relinquish them. You can have them back after you finish. Remember, God knows your emotional state without your having to tell Him. Just read this prayer as a basic statement of fact, a simple but heartfelt request.

Here it is:

Dear God, thank You for bringing me to a point in my life where I realize that I need the kind of help only You can provide. Despite the weight of my problems, at least I am no longer living under the delusion that I am self-sufficient. I know I need a miracle right now, and I know I must come to You to obtain it. I stand before You empty-handed, filled with faith, hope, and love, to humbly ask for the following miracle: [State your request].

Filled with praise and gratitude, I pray for this miracle with my words, mind, heart, and soul for Your greater honor and glory. Amen.

I know this prayer might seem easy, but believe me, it's powerful!

We'll be adding more to it at the end of each chapter. But resist the temptation to skip ahead—even if you badly need a miracle. What we're doing is laying the foundation for an authentic, sincere, comprehensive miracle prayer; one that is not gimmicky or superstitious in any way but is theologically sound.

Remember, this is only the beginning part of the prayer, but the beginning is oh so important—especially if you say it calmly and with even the smallest measure of hope.

Yes, hope. Where there's life, there's hope. As long as you're breathing, there's hope. As long as you can pray, there's hope. Never forget that. God knew from all eternity that you would need a miracle right now and that you'd be reading these words. Moreover, He knew these words would give you hope. And God can neither deceive nor be deceived.

So be of good cheer and try not to be afraid! You're already on your way to obtaining something miraculous.

2

Just What Is a Miracle?

If you want to obtain a miracle, you must first understand what a miracle is.

The word "miracle" has two meanings: a strict definition and a more casual, generic use. It is similar with other words, such as "legend," which, strictly defined, is a traditional story or myth, often about a historical figure, that has been passed down through generations. In everyday conversation, however, people might refer to anyone as a "legend" if he or she is exceptionally good at something—for instance, a famous athlete. The same is true of the words "hero," "genius," and "masterpiece." Each of these words has a strict definition and also a more casual use.

So it is with "miracle."

The definition of "miracle" is an extraordinary occurrence, perceivable to our senses, that causes wonder and amazement. It comes from the Latin word *miraculum*, which means "something wonderful" or "a marvel." More importantly, a miracle is the result of some hidden, divine intervention in the natural order of things, either directly by God or by one of His agents—such as an angel or a human being. These interventions usually do not violate the laws of nature; rather, they are *beyond* those laws, or they *supplement* or *intensify* them in some mysterious way.[2]

Such a distinction might seem small, but it's quite important. God respects the laws of nature. After all, He created them. He created the universe and everything in it, including the laws that govern it. He created the laws of physics. He created the laws of chemistry. He created the laws of human physiology. When He interferes with these laws and performs a miracle, He doesn't often break them blatantly by suspending the natural order; instead,

---

[2] Karl Rahner, *Theological Dictionary*, trans. Richard Strachan (New York: Herder and Herder, 1965), 342–345; Thomas Aquinas, *ST*, I-II, q. 110, art. 4; *Merriam-Webster's Collegiate Dictionary*, 11th ed. (Springfield, MA: Merriam-Webster, 2003), s.v. "miracle"; Charlton T. Lewis and Charles Short, *A Latin Dictionary* (Oxford: Clarendon Press, 1879), s.v. "miraculum."

He interacts with them in a way that changes the outcome of a particular situation.

That sounds complicated, but human beings do something similar all the time. If the weather is cold and rainy, we don't try to magically raise the temperature before leaving our homes. What we do is put on a coat and hat to keep us warm and dry. Thus, we "interfere" with nature, in a manner of speaking, but we don't break any meteorological laws. We simply use our abilities to supplement nature and change the outcome. For example, humans have devised a way to fly through the sky using airplanes and helicopters, but we've accomplished this extraordinary feat by taking advantage of the natural laws of aerodynamics, not by contradicting the law of gravity. Humans have also found ways to treat coronary valve disease, not by contradicting the laws of physiology but by supplementing them with the introduction of various kinds of artificial valves.

Well, God has much greater power than we do, and consequently, He has a much greater ability to supplement the laws of nature to achieve His aims. For instance, in the Bible and throughout history, there are numerous examples of people who have been exposed to intense heat and fire and yet, because of their prayers, have not only survived but have not even been burned.[3] How could that be? Obviously, miracles were involved. But when God performed those miracles, He didn't change any of the laws of chemical combustion. He didn't use any form of wizardry to eliminate the heat that comes naturally from fire. Rather, He most likely protected those people by surrounding them with some kind of mystical fireproof covering of His own design—just as we use our human powers to put on a jacket to protect us from the cold or to put on fire-protective gloves to protect us from intense heat. In other words, those miracles involved no infraction of the laws of nature, just a displacement. As C. S. Lewis put it: "The divine art of miracles is not an art of suspending the pattern to which events conform but of feeding new events into the pattern."[4]

Thus, when Moses parted the Red Sea in the book of Exodus, God didn't necessarily violate the laws of physics and marine biology by making a whole tract of water magically disappear. Instead, He may have simply introduced a "new event" into the pattern of nature—perhaps sudden, unexplainable winds or a supernatural phenomenon that

---

[3] See, for example, Daniel 3:19–27.
[4] C. S. Lewis, *Miracles: A Preliminary Study* (New York: Macmillan, 1947), 93.

had the effect of displacing the water of the Red Sea in such a way that the Israelites were able to walk along its seabed.

This doesn't mean that God *can't* break the laws of nature when He performs miracles.

God can do anything He wants. And certainly, that is the case with some of the miraculous actions of Christ in the Gospels—most notably His own Resurrection, something completely out of the realm of natural events or powers. But it's not something He usually does. It's not His preferred way of performing miracles.

Why is this fact so important? Because it's a key to understanding the mind of God. God created the physical universe in a certain way and with a certain purpose. He governs that universe, in part, through various physical laws of nature. The result is a marvelously delicate, beautiful, stable, and harmonious place. Similarly, God created another realm of existence called the supernatural world. This is the world of the spiritual, the world of Heaven and the angels and grace. These two realities—the natural and the supernatural—can and do interact at times, but only under the governing providence of God.

The bottom line is that God is a God of order. He takes His creation seriously. When He wants to work a miracle, He doesn't reach down into the world with His divine hand and violently break all the natural laws as if He were a thief breaking into a jewelry cabinet. He respects those laws and interferes with them only when He has good reason and only with infinite care and in certain specified ways. He's not a magician or a conjurer or a wizard. He's a loving Father who supplements the natural laws with his supernatural power in a very elegant, seamless, purposeful, and pastoral way.

In fact, true miracles occur far less frequently than even religious people think. An actual, bona fide miracle—according to the strict definition of the word—necessarily involves unexplainable supernatural activity, such as protection from fire, or the restoration of sight to someone who is blind, or the overnight disappearance of a massive malignant tumor, or the parting of the seas, or the raising of the dead. For something to qualify as a miracle according to theological standards, it must not be explainable by natural causes, no matter how extraordinary.

Indeed, when presented with a possible miracle—such as those investigated to advance the cause of someone's canonization—the Catholic Church always starts with the presumption that a miracle has *not* occurred and that the person making the claim for it is either mistaken, ignorant, self-deceived, or, in the worst case, trying to deceive others. It is only after an examination of the facts—often conducted by a bishop and a special commission of scientists and other experts—that a determination is provided to the competent ecclesiastic authority as to whether the alleged miracle is "worthy of belief." And this investigation is often long and rigorous and includes an assessment of the mental health of the person making the claim, the possibility that there could be a human explanation, the possibility that the event could have diabolical origins, and a study of the "good fruit" that has resulted from the occurrence.[5]

In other words, the Church starts with a healthy dose of skepticism when investigating any alleged supernatural occurrence and utilizes several objective, verifiable criteria to determine its legitimacy.

Thus, if a man is in danger of losing his home because he is in debt and suddenly wins a million dollars in a lottery,

---

[5] Tia Ghose, "The Science of Miracles: How the Vatican Decides," Live Science, July 9, 2013, https://www.livescience.com/38033-how-vatican-identifies-miracles.html; Sabrina Ferrisi, "How Does the Catholic Church Investigate Eucharistic Miracles?" *National Catholic Register*, June 11, 2023, https://www.ncregister.com/features/how-does-the-catholic-church-investigate-eucharistic-miracles.

that would not be considered a miracle because it is explainable by natural causes. Or, if someone has been given a diagnosis of terminal cancer and then, against all odds, the cancer goes into remission, that, too, is not a true miracle because the phenomenon of remission does not necessarily involve the supernatural. It might just be that the medical treatment worked, despite the doctor's predictions.

Does that mean that God didn't have a hand in these events, or that they didn't come about as a result of prayer? Of course not. God certainly did have a hand in them, and prayer absolutely did play a role. The difference between such unlikely occurrences and genuine miracles is that God answered these prayers by allowing events to unfold in a natural way. Yes, He orchestrated them, but they all have perfectly rational, scientifically acceptable explanations. There was no need to supplement the natural law with supernatural power, as God did in parting the Red Sea or in protecting His prophets from fire or in restoring sight to the blind.

And this brings us to the more generic definition of the word "miracle": something extraordinary that happens *as a result of prayer* but is explainable by natural events and by *secondary* causes.

When God uses secondary causes, it means only that He doesn't intervene directly in the natural order to achieve His objective. Instead, He draws the rest of us into His providential design to influence events. In other words, He uses people—our family members, friends, teachers, doctors, therapists, lawyers, bankers, construction workers, or even complete strangers. Indeed, this has been God's plan of salvation from the beginning of the world: to use *us* to help save *us*. It's the normal way He speaks to us too: not through some miraculous booming voice from the heavens but through His prophets, the moral law, the Church, the Bible, the inspiration of angels, the workings of the physical universe, the events that take place in our lives, and answered prayers.

St. Thomas Aquinas said that our prayers are a means through which God has ordained certain effects. In other words, our prayers do not change God's will but "help" His will come to pass. God uses our prayers, like our actions, to assist Him in carrying forward His divine plan.[6]

The point is that, from all eternity, God has seen your prayers—including your present request for a miracle—and He has taken them into account when arranging reality. Indeed, sometimes God will allow certain things to come

---

[6] Thomas Aquinas, *ST*, II-II, q. 83, art. 2; Karlo Broussard, "Does Prayer Change God's Mind?" *Catholic Answers Magazine*, June 6, 2016.

to pass only *if* you have prayed for them. If you have *not* prayed for them, they will *not* come to pass. Therefore, your prayers have value in the same way that your actions have value. They really can work because God has chosen to use them in the grand scheme of His divine plan.

At this very moment, all around the world, prayers are being answered in amazing ways. People might use the word "miraculous" to describe these phenomena because the hand of God is so apparent in them, but in most cases, God achieves His purposes without intervening in events with His supernatural power. Instead, He achieves His purposes by arranging all our free choices, prayers, and actions in a natural way—in other words, without recourse to bona fide miracles. That's the way God generally goes about answering prayers—including requests for miracles.

So, if you're battling terminal cancer and the treatment works, that's really an answered prayer, not a miracle. If you have a son who has been hooked on heroin for a decade and suddenly finds a rehab program that works, that's really an answered prayer, not a miracle. If you're facing a major financial crisis and, through a series of "lucky" breaks, somehow manage to avoid losing your house and your business, that's really an answered prayer, not a miracle. If your marriage and family have been falling apart and a last-ditch attempt at therapy results in a stunning and unexpected improvement, that's really an answered prayer, not a miracle.

And this is the real solution to the riddle I posed in chapter 1. Are miracles rare, or do they happen every day? The answer depends on what kind of "miracle" we're talking about. Bona fide miracles—authenticated divine interventions in the laws of nature, such as the overnight disappearance of a malignant tumor without any kind of treatment—are indeed very rare. But extraordinary answers to prayer that *seem* miraculous are very common. Indeed, they happen every minute of the day, in every corner of the globe.

I know this can be confusing. But what I'm saying here really boils down to one point: Authentic miracles always involve some kind of supernatural intervention by God in the natural order. Answers to prayer—even extraordinary ones—do not.

Of course, if you're reading this book, you may not care about this theological distinction—whether God grants you an actual miracle that meets the rigorous criteria of the Church or whether He simply orchestrates events so that what happens only seems miraculous. As long as you get the result you want, you'll be happy.

If that's the case, we're on the same page. For the purpose of this book, we are going to treat the two types of "miraculous" events the same—not only miracles that can be approved by the Vatican but any kind of event that's "not supposed to happen," given the laws of statistics.

We're also going to employ a strategy.

The famous football coach Vince Lombardi used to urge his players to chase "perfection" relentlessly, knowing full well that they would never attain it. But in chasing perfection, he assured them, they would catch "excellence."[7]

We're going to try something similar in this book. In the next chapter, we'll be talking about some of Christ's miracle "promises" in the Bible. These promises were often made by Christ after He performed bona fide, authentic miracles according to the strict definition of the word. We'll see that whenever Christ worked miracles, there were usually various conditions that needed to be fulfilled, or at least elements that had to be in place—such as faith or trust or persistence or the desire for God's greater glory.

Our approach in this book will be to fulfill every single one of these conditions for a bona fide miracle, understanding that God will probably not perform one for us.

---

[7] Vince Lombardi, quoted in Chuck Carlson, *Game of My Life: 25 Stories of Packers Football* (Champaign, IL: Sports Publishing, 2004), 149.

But in "chasing" a true miracle—and really praying that we might get one—we will be hoping at the same time to "catch" an extraordinary answer to our prayers. In other words, we're going to do everything we can to obtain God's miraculous intervention in the laws of nature in hopes that God, seeing our faithful attempt, will at least give us an answer to prayer.

Remember, our belief in miracles starts with the belief in creation. Before the act of Creation, there was nothing. After it, there was everything, including the laws of the universe. Reflect on that mind-boggling truth for a moment, and then recall the specific miracle you're asking God to perform. No matter how difficult you think it might be for Him, it is truly *infinitesimal* compared with the act of Creation. Even a bona fide, biblical miracle such as the parting of the Red Sea is nothing to God. As a priest I know said, God created all the oceans of the world, so it's no big deal for Him to move a little water around!

Keep that in mind as we go forward in our exploration of the miraculous. Try to have a childlike attitude and believe that, for God, nothing is impossible and that He has wanted from all eternity to answer your request with a miraculous gift.

In the meantime, add the following petition to the prayer we learned in chapter 1, immediately following your specific request:

Lord, I know that You created the universe and the laws that govern it, and that nothing You do contradicts that order. Help me to recognize Your hand in all that unfolds, whether miraculous or not, and help me especially to trust in Your divine plan.

3
The Miracle Paradoxes

I have a friend who has been a Catholic priest in New Jersey for close to forty years. His name is Fr. Brian, and miracles seem to follow him wherever he goes. In fact, I call him the "miracle priest." Fr. Brian is a very mild-mannered man, very unassuming and humble, the furthest thing in the world from the fire-and-brimstone type. But he believes in the power of prayer as much as any Evangelical preacher or faith healer.

About fifteen years ago, a woman in Fr. Brian's parish gave birth to a baby boy with serious health problems. One of his kidneys wasn't functioning, and the other had started to shut down. The baby was in the NICU at the hospital and was not expected to survive. The parents asked Fr. Brian to pray for a miracle.

At the very same time, a man in Fr. Brian's parish was suffering from terminal cancer. He had been a kind, soft-spoken individual his whole life, but he did not deal with his illness gracefully. He had become extremely embittered and hostile and verbally abusive to his wife and family. It was very unlike him, but, of course, the fear of death can turn a person's emotions upside down. Anyway, Fr. Brian went to the man's house at the request of his wife and tried to talk to him. In the course of their conversation, Fr. Brian happened to tell the man about the baby in the hospital who was struggling for life. Then Fr. Brian was inspired to make a bold suggestion. He said to the sick man, "Why don't you offer up your suffering for that little baby?" Taken aback, the man thought for a moment and then, surprisingly, said he would. Even more surprisingly, the man's agitated behavior immediately stopped. He no longer acted short-tempered and abusive but, instead, went back to being the gentle, soft-spoken man he had always been.

Soon afterward, the man died. He did not receive a miraculous cure for his terminal illness. But he had surrendered his will to the Lord, and despite his terrible physical pain, he was able to die calmly, courageously, and with a peace that "transcends all understanding" (Phil. 4:7). The really interesting thing, however, is that, just after the man's funeral, Fr. Brian received a call from the mother of the baby. She was crying. Fr. Brian let out a sigh, expecting to be told that the child had died. But he soon realized that the woman was crying tears of joy rather than sorrow. Not only had her baby's kidney stopped shutting down, but his other kidney—the one that had not been working since birth—had amazingly started to function. Such a dramatic reversal was medically remarkable. The doctors were at a loss. They couldn't explain this sudden "renal function recovery" *and* "restoration" in a baby on the verge of death.

But the story doesn't end there. Many years later, Fr. Brian was giving a Confirmation retreat to a group of eighth graders. During one of the talks, he told the students about this miracle, in order to impress upon them the power of the Holy Spirit—which they would be receiving in a special way in the sacrament of Confirmation. After Fr. Brian had finished speaking, a strapping, healthy young teenager came bounding up to the podium, excitedly saying, "Father, I'm the little boy who was in the hospital! I'm the one whose kidneys started working again. My parents have been telling me for years about how I survived, but I never knew any of the details. But it's me!"

This story contains so many mysterious paradoxes of faith: the sick man's acceptance and offering of suffering are what restored peace to him; in his weakest moment, he found the strength to help someone else through the power of sacrifice; his death coincided with the baby's miraculous recovery. These apparent incongruities remind us that peace can come through pain, strength through weakness, and life through death.

Indeed, the more we learn about life and Christian spirituality and the theology of miracles, the more we see the importance of the concept of paradoxes.

A paradox is an idea that *seems* self-contradictory or logically absurd and yet is not. When examined more closely, it reveals a deeper truth about life. For example, the statement "less is more" seems like a contradiction in terms, but in reality, it perfectly summarizes the truth that something done in a simple way often conveys more truth or beauty than something done in a complicated way—even though the complicated version might comprise more components. Likewise, "less is more" can also mean that having too many options can be a bad thing because it can lead to anxiety and indecision and even paralysis. In other words, if having "more" means that nothing gets done, then "more" is truly less.

There are many paradoxes in life. For instance: the only constant is change; the exception proves the rule;

the more you give, the more you get; the closer you look, the less you see; the more you know, the more you realize how ignorant you are. And on and on.

Indeed, the whole of Christian theology is built on paradoxes: God is one, but God is three. Jesus Christ is fully God yet fully man. The first shall be last, and the last shall be first. You must lose your life to gain it. At the very heart of Catholic spirituality is a paradox too: the Eucharist has the appearance, taste, texture, and molecular structure of bread and wine, but, in substance, it is the Body and Blood, Soul and Divinity of Jesus Christ.

G. K. Chesterton, who was famous for using paradoxes, asserted that they have the power to reveal deeper truths because they are rooted in the belief that human understanding is limited and finite, while the reality of life and creation reflects the infinite nature of God. Since there's no way that something finite, such as our intellects, can fully comprehend something infinite, such as God, there are bound to be times when what we discover about life seems to be a contradiction, and the only way we can understand that discovery is to embrace the apparent contradiction.[8]

---

[8] G. K. Chesterton, *Orthodoxy* (New York: John Lane, 1908), 65–66.

Chesterton illustrated this idea through various examples, one of which involved the perception of a person's height. He explained that a very short person might see another person as tall, while a giant might see the same person as short. The truth is that the person being viewed is neither very tall nor very short but average. His size depends on the height from which he is seen by others. In other words, the contradiction arises purely because different observers are looking at the subject from different angles.[9]

The same holds true when it comes to understanding the reality of God. To limited human beings like you and me, God is able to express His truth only in fragments. Those fragments of the overall truth sometimes seem at odds with each other, when, in fact, they are part of a cohesive whole. Chesterton argued that paradoxes force us to look beyond the superficial and seek a more profound unity. This approach not only enriches our spiritual and intellectual lives but can also startle us into seeing the essence of faith, where mystery and understanding coexist. It has been said that paradoxes "stand truth on its head" in order to attract our attention. In other words,

[9] Chesterton, *Orthodoxy*, 88.

the deeper truth behind paradoxes lies in their ability, like a many-sided mirror, to reflect the infinite complexity of life, created by an infinite God.

Which brings us back to the subject of miracles.

In the last two chapters, we spoke about the fact that miracles are, by definition, rare, yet they happen every day. Based on what we just discussed, it should be apparent that this is not a real contradiction but simply a paradox. The deeper truth revealed in this statement is that bona fide miracles are infrequent, but "miraculous" answers to prayer are extremely common and are built into God's providential plan.

The purpose of this book is to show you how best to tap into that plan. And the way we're going to begin is by looking at some of the things Jesus Christ said about miracles in the Gospels. Predictably, we're going to see that much of what He said was paradoxical in nature, and our hope is that, by embracing these paradoxes, we might receive either a bona fide miracle or at least an extraordinary answer to our prayers.

Now, in reading the New Testament, we discover Jesus performing many incredible signs, such as healings, exorcisms, and "nature miracles" (e.g., calming the storm or walking on water). The healings normally involve a direct encounter between Christ and the person being healed, generally through a request for a cure and an act of faith on the part of the recipient. Indeed, a careful review of these accounts reveals several "conditions" that often precede Christ's divine interventions. It's important to note that these are not hard-and-fast conditions. Sometimes they are not clearly present but are merely implied. Sometimes Christ goes out of His way to perform miracles without demanding any prerequisites. But it's true enough to say that, in the great majority of cases, there were at least contributing factors that influenced Christ's decision to perform a miracle and that therefore pertain to our own miracle quest.

We're going to discuss these contributing factors in this book, but for now I'd like to focus on a few of the explicit miracle "promises" made by God, in the person of Christ.

Without any explanatory comments (we'll get to those soon enough), here are the words of the Son of God, direct and unembellished, as recorded in the New Testament. Please take your time to read them over slowly and carefully:

❖ "Ask and it will be given to you; seek and you will find; knock and the door will be opened to you. For everyone who asks receives; the one who seeks finds; and to the one who knocks, the door will be opened" (Matt. 7:7–8; Luke 11:9–10).

* "Truly, I tell you, if you have faith as small as a mustard seed, you can say to this mountain, 'Move from here to there,' and it will move. Nothing will be impossible for you" (Matt. 17:20).

* "Again I say to you, if two of you agree on earth about anything they ask, it will be done for them by my Father in heaven. For where two or three are gathered in my name, there am I in the midst of them" (Matt. 18:19–20, RSVCE).

* "Truly I tell you, if you have faith and do not doubt ... you can say to this mountain, 'Go, throw yourself into the sea,' and it will be done. If you believe, you will receive whatever you ask for in prayer" (Matt. 21:21–22).

* "Everything is possible for one who believes" (Mark 9:23).

* "Therefore I tell you, whatever you ask for in prayer, believe that you have received it, and it will be yours" (Mark 11:24).

* "If you have faith as small as a mustard seed, you can say to this mulberry tree, 'Be uprooted

and planted in the sea,' and it will obey you"
(Luke 17:6).

- ❖ "Whatever you ask in my name, I will do it, that
  the Father may be glorified in the Son; if you
  ask anything in my name, I will do it" (John
  14:13–14, RSVCE).
- ❖ "If you remain in me and my words remain in
  you, ask whatever you wish, and it will be done
  for you" (John 15:7).

No matter what denomination or faith tradition in
Christianity you happen to follow, I'm sure you'll agree
that these promises all seem straightforward and powerful.
They are clear assurances—made by God Himself—that
if people behave or believe in a certain way, He will do
incredibly miraculous things for them.

Even more impressive is that these promises were fulfilled—in abundance—not only during Jesus' ministry but
in the years and decades following Christ's time on earth.
Indeed, the time of the early Church is often referred to
as the "Age of Miracles." During this period (as vividly
recounted in the Acts of the Apostles), miracles weren't
rare occurrences; they were everyday realities. Healings,
raising of the dead, exorcisms, divine interventions, and

miraculous signs weren't the exceptions; they were the rule. Not only did faith in Christ result in spontaneous acts of wonder; the community itself was deeply connected to the source of miraculous power through its prayer life. As a result, miracles abounded.

And these events extended beyond the apostolic era. Irenaeus, an early Church Father, asserts that healings were common among believers. The writings of Justin Martyr also reflect this reality, defending the legitimacy of miracles as signs of God's involvement with His people.[10] Paraphrasing Chesterton: early Christians lived not just in a world filled with miracles but in a miraculous world.[11]

Why were there so many miracles? Augustine of Hippo, in his work *The City of God*, argued that miracles were necessary to establish the Faith during its beginning stages. Thomas Aquinas, in his *Summa Theologica*, said that early miracles were meant to demonstrate the truth of Christian doctrine.[12] In other words, it makes sense that God

---

[10] Irenaeus, *Against Heresies* 2.32.4, in *The Ante-Nicene Fathers*, ed. Alexander Roberts and James Donaldson, vol. 1 (Buffalo: Christian Literature, 1885), 428; Justin Martyr, *Dialogue with Trypho* 7, in *The Ante-Nicene Fathers*, vol. 1, 199.

[11] See Chesterton, *Orthodoxy*, 88.

[12] *ST*, III, q. 43.

would perform an increased number of miracles during this period to help "jump-start" the nascent religion. It was necessary that the institution of the Church become strong enough to hand the Faith down to future generations, sacramentally.[13] Once that institution was firmly established, the need for astonishing signs diminished, and so the Age of Miracles came to an end relatively early in post-apostolic times. Miracles themselves have continued to occur throughout history and up until the present day, but not even the most fervent believer would claim that modern Christians have been blessed with the same kind of extraordinary and unprecedented outpouring of the Holy Spirit as was experienced by their early Christian forebears. It's clear from simple observation that requests for miracles today—even from the saintliest people—are often denied, or at least seem to be denied.

Case in point: a good friend of mine belongs to a close-knit Evangelical community. Several years ago, a young girl in his congregation, only six years old, was diagnosed with a terminal illness. This tragedy prompted the

[13] Augustine, *The City of God*, trans. Marcus Dods (New York: Random House, 1950), 22.8; Thomas Aquinas, *ST*, I-II, q. 105, art. 8.

entire church to rally in support of the girl and her family through fervent intercessory prayer. The congregation engaged in extended communal prayer and held weekly worship services and healing services. They prayed over the girl in Jesus' name. They even thanked the Lord in advance for the anticipated healing, as Mark 11:24 instructs.

Despite their unwavering faith and exhaustive spiritual efforts, the young girl's condition did not improve. But as she deteriorated, something interesting happened. The faithful members of the congregation became *more* confident in her imminent cure. They intensified their praying, sang even louder, and praised and thanked the Lord even more. They whipped themselves into a kind of spiritual-emotional frenzy. They were convinced with 100 percent certitude that this little girl was going to be cured. They didn't entertain a single doubt in their minds. They knew she would be healed because they knew their faith was strong enough to "move mountains."

Well, the little girl died, just as her doctors had predicted. And it's not an exaggeration to say that her passing left the community devastated. Yes, the people were upset about her tragic death, but something else had happened as well. Their faith was shaken. Some members even left the church, and those who stayed had to grapple with profound questions about the nature of faith, the efficacy of prayer, and the will of God.

What went wrong? The community had literally embodied not only Jesus' miracle promises but also the scriptural command to "pray for each other that you may be healed" (James 5:16) and to "pray in the Spirit on all occasions with all kinds of prayers and requests" (Eph. 6:18). Why hadn't they been granted their miracle? Did they lack faith? Did they pray in an incorrect manner?

I have a story like this too. I don't usually like telling personal stories — especially sad ones. In fact, whenever I read an author who describes some traumatic personal event in graphic detail, I tend to cringe. It's not that I object to sharing; it's just not how I approach my writing or my life. I prefer to keep my private life private. I'm going to make some exceptions in this book, however, because my experiences fit in with what I'm trying to communicate and because they might help you.

I was very close to my father. He was by far the most influential person in my life, shaping almost all my thoughts, beliefs, tastes, and views. In his early seventies, he was diagnosed with a deadly blood disorder. Despite consultations with top-notch specialists in New York City, the unanimous verdict was grim: he had about a year to live, maybe a year and a half if he was lucky. The only treatment was weekly blood transfusions.

The diagnosis and everything related to my father's medical care was extremely difficult for my family. But as a committed Catholic, I believed in miracles and in God's power to do the impossible. So I began praying and enlisting the help of God. To say I tried everything would be an understatement. I said novenas, attended daily Mass as frequently as I could, said my Rosary every day, and prayed myriad devotions. And these weren't just rote prayers. They were impassioned pleas. My family and I went through a great deal of turmoil. One of my brothers, a priest, regularly said Masses for my father.

Interestingly, my request to God wasn't for a complete healing; I accepted my father's terminal diagnosis. What I wanted was more time. And not even a lot more. Instead of a year and a half, I asked God for two or three years—just a bit more than what the doctors predicted. Surely, with all the prayers, Masses, novenas, and Rosaries, I thought, God would grant us this tiny request—which really amounted to just a few more months.

But guess what happened? My father died exactly fifteen months after his diagnosis, not even making it to the year-and-a-half mark. To make matters worse, it was not a pretty death. What went wrong? Was it my lack of faith? Was it some insincerity in my prayers? Why hadn't God granted us even this comparatively modest miracle? It's a question that haunted me for a long time.

I'm sure you have your own sad stories. There's just no way around it. God sometimes refuses the miracles we ask for, even when we have faith and even when we try to follow the commands of the Gospels. It's a perplexing problem. God's miracle promises are certainly there—numerous, clear, and, most importantly, without an expiration date. They emphatically assert that miracles—or at least extraordinary answers to prayers—aren't just possible but are part of the fabric of life. If we pray for something with faith, there's no reason we shouldn't receive it. That's certainly what the Bible seems to indicate. Yet we know from experience that it's often not the case.

I believe the solution lies in the fact that these miracle promises of Christ, while appearing to be straightforward, are often misunderstood. In fact, I believe it's more accurate to call these promises of Christ "miracle paradoxes." When we analyze them carefully, as we will in the following pages, we'll see that these promises don't require that we fulfill only one condition but, rather, that we embrace several seemingly contradictory positions simultaneously.

This can be confusing. To hold contradictory ideas in your head and to implement them in your life requires not only a delicate balance but also an attempt to move in "opposite" directions or to switch rapidly back and forth between ideas. In fact, it's a little like riding a seesaw at a playground. A seesaw has two opposite ends. If you put all your weight on one end, that end of the seesaw will stay in the same "down" position. But if you exert force on the other side too, the seesaw will start moving and energy will be generated.

Likewise with paradoxes. If you focus on only one part, you'll have only a one-sided understanding of the truth. And that's what happens quite often. Sometimes your personality type or your psychology or even your gifts can dispose you to favoring one side of God's truth. But if you try very hard to grasp and embrace *both* parts of the paradox at the *same* time, you'll achieve a proper balance and also create the kind of spiritual power you need to discover even more truth and perhaps even to perform the miraculous.

Briefly, then, here are seven Bible-based pairs of ideas that have been traditionally associated with obtaining miracles. At first glance, they may seem to contradict themselves, but they do not. They are merely paradoxical, and their purpose is to reveal deeper truths about the interplay between the human and the divine, the natural and the supernatural:

1. The spontaneous petitions we bring to God in prayer versus the true desires of our souls
2. The benefit of fear and tribulation versus the need for courage
3. The value of persistent prayer versus the need to have a decisive faith
4. The obligation to be self-reliant versus the need to surrender to God
5. The idea of dying to ourselves versus the idea of living fully and truly
6. The centrality of a personal relationship with Jesus versus the need to be part of a community of believers
7. The benefit of being clear and precise in our prayers versus the need to be completely open to the will of God

For the remainder of this book, we're going to be examining these seven "miracle paradoxes" one at a time.

I want to assure you that the last thing I intend to do is toy with your emotions by making false claims that you can magically obtain a miracle *if you do "x."* This book is not about superstition. There's never any guarantee that a miracle will happen. But I sincerely believe that if you attempt to truly understand these paradoxes and to embrace and implement them in your life, you'll be in a much stronger position to receive the miraculous answer to prayer that you so earnestly desire.

In the meantime, add the following petition to the prayer you've been saying:

Lord, help me embrace in faith the deeper truths that are revealed through Your divine paradoxes.

4

Spoken Prayer versus Soul Prayer

The most obvious "condition" that needs to be fulfilled if you want a miracle is that you have to ask for one!

Of course, it's true that sometimes other people can ask *for* you. We see several instances of this in the Gospels, as when the friends of a paralytic man lower him through a roof to Jesus (Luke 5:17–28), or when Martha and Mary ask Jesus to help their dying brother, Lazarus (John 11:1–24), or when a man in the crowd begs Jesus to exorcise his demon-possessed son (Mark 9:14–29). Even in these cases, however, there is always an implicit request from the person who needs the miracle, and the only reason he doesn't ask for one himself is that he is physically unable to do so.

Thus, if you need a miracle, you must first humble yourself to ask God for help. Most times, this isn't an obstacle, unless you're really a hardened atheist. Nevertheless, there are times when asking for a miracle can be problematic—even for a fervent believer. The reason is that many of us have a misunderstanding about what it means to "ask" in the first place. Many of us don't realize that asking God for something in prayer involves another paradox: the heartfelt desires we express in prayer are not always in line with the true desires of our souls. As Jeremiah 17:9 tells us: "The heart is deceitful above all things."

Let's take this slowly because it's critical to our understanding of miracles, and while it might seem a simple concept to grasp, sometimes even the most intelligent theologians get muddled when discussing it.

It is often said that God gives us what we need, not what we want. Indeed, that maxim is true, to some extent. Plenty of examples come to mind. A person in a tumultuous relationship prays for his partner to never leave him, but breaking up might be the healthiest option for both parties. What he really needs is to exit the relationship as soon as possible and begin a new chapter in his life. A man in debt prays to win the lottery to solve his financial difficulties, but if he wins, he might indulge in more reckless spending and eventually find himself deeper in debt with serious legal problems as well. What he really needs is to learn how to budget his money, despite the hardships he faces. A woman seeking a job prays for a position at a prestigious company, but upon getting it, she realizes that the company's culture clashes with her values, and she consequently feels stressed and unfulfilled and ends up quitting. What she really needs is to identify the type of job that is best suited to her personality and to risk getting rejected many times until she finds it.

None of these people see that what they are praying for conflicts with what they need. So, yes, the idea that God sees the bigger picture and knows that what we need is often at odds with what we want, is valid and understandable. And yet, when we rattle off this cliché—as spiritual people often do—it somehow doesn't console us. In fact, it paints a picture of a God who doesn't care very much about our most intense desires but cares only about the things that will benefit us in the long run. And that makes God seem a bit pedantic—sort of like a stern, distant doctor with a bad bedside manner, focused only on symptoms and test results—and not the loving parent He claims to be. Imagine a child on a sweltering summer day who asks his father for an ice-cream cone, and the father's response is: "Well, Johnny, I don't care what you want. What you need is something healthy. So here's a serving of steamed spinach instead."

Is that who God is?

There's got to be more to prayer than God's simply giving us what we need. And the key, I think, lies in the fact that, most times, what we ask for in prayer isn't so clear-cut and simple as a child's request for an ice-cream cone on a hot day. In fact, many times, when we ask for something in prayer, we not only don't need it, but we don't *want* it either.

Let me explain.

What does the woman who is praying for a job at a prestigious company really want? Does she want that specific job, or does she want what she *thinks* that job will give her? Perhaps she thinks the new position will give her a certain social significance. Perhaps she thinks it will help her advance her career. Perhaps she thinks it will increase her salary, which, in turn, will give her more financial freedom. Perhaps she thinks the job will bring her enjoyment. Those are all the things she wants—not the position itself. The position is merely a vehicle to deliver the emotions she wants to feel—significance, accomplishment, financial freedom, pleasure, and so forth. Those are the things she is *really* praying for. If she knew that obtaining the job would do exactly the opposite of what she hoped, she obviously wouldn't ask for it.

Many times, we say we know what we want, but we don't—because we're not looking deeper than our immediate desires, and we're not giving any thought to what lies beyond the words we're using to articulate those desires.

So receiving what we ask for in prayer isn't simply about needs versus wants. It's about the fact that, when we pray to God, He doesn't just hear the words that are coming out of our mouths. He hears what we truly desire in our souls.

Perhaps a young athlete praying for an Olympic gold medal is really asking God to be seen as exceptional and worthy of admiration; perhaps a father praying for his child to be accepted into a prestigious university is really asking God to make sure his child is successful in life. Perhaps a mother praying for a miraculous cure for her daughter's cancer is really asking God for more than even she knows—she's asking God for her daughter to live and be happy forever; for her to never, ever die.

The truth is that, most times, we don't know for sure what we want. We experience some kind of problem in life, and in response we feel either fear or desire. Then we try to identify a solution to the problem that will squelch that fear or fulfill that desire. If we believe God has the power to help us, we naturally try to involve Him in the solution we've come up with. And *that's* what we end up praying for—the specific solution we've identified to help us deal with our fears and desires. We pronounce the words of our prayer; we hear ourselves saying those words, and we really believe that we mean them. But we're mistaken. We've been fooled because we haven't thought things through. We haven't discerned the deeper truth. Instead, we've given our desires and our fears a superficial interpretation and come up with a superficial solution.

God doesn't do that. He doesn't take us at our word. He's not fooled by what comes out of our mouths. To answer our prayers in the most meaningful and significant way possible, He pays us the great honor of looking past our words to the most profound longings of our souls. *Those* are the prayers He considers granting—the real ones; the ones we actually want answered.

Let's look again at the most well-known miracle promise in the Bible and see if Christ confirms this point. But this time let's read the whole passage, and not just the famous first lines:

Ask and it will be given to you; seek and you will find; knock and the door will be opened to you. For everyone who asks receives; the one who seeks finds; and to the one who knocks, the door will be opened. Which of you, if your son asks for bread, will give him a stone? Or if he asks for a fish, will give him a snake? If you, then, though you are evil, know how to give good gifts to your children, how much more will your Father in heaven give good gifts to those who ask him! (Matt. 7:7–11)

The Gospel of Luke repeats this promise, but with some slight variations:

Which of you fathers, if your son asks for a fish, will give him a snake instead? Or if he asks for an egg, will give him a scorpion? If you then, though you are evil, know how to give good gifts to your children, how much more will your Father in heaven give the Holy Spirit to those who ask him! (Luke 11:11–13)

One of the keys to solving the problem of unanswered miracle requests and unanswered prayer in general is contained in these Bible verses. Jesus initially states, in language strikingly bold and unambiguous, that God will say yes to anyone who asks, seeks, and knocks. But then He immediately follows up with some rather strange questions:

"Which of you," He says, "if your son asks for bread, will give him a stone? Or if he asks for a fish will give him a snake? Or if he asks for an egg, will give him a scorpion?"

These questions aren't exactly non sequiturs, but neither do they flow naturally from the assurance that everyone who asks, seeks, and knocks will be answered. The only way they really make sense is if Christ means exactly what we've been arguing in this chapter—that people often don't know what they're praying for.

What Christ is saying here is that He is going to answer all our prayers in the affirmative, but He is going to give us only what we truly pray for, what we truly want—not those things we *say* we want because we have falsely interpreted our feelings.

And when we look back at the "unanswered" prayers in our lives, isn't this what we often find to be the case?

My goodness, when I think of all the things in my life that I prayed for, I want to get down on my knees and thank God for not giving them to me. I know now that I did *not* want what I so earnestly begged for. I wanted other things—things I was too ignorant to understand, or too lazy to discover for myself through self-reflection, or too sinful to see through spiritual discernment, or too clumsy to articulate correctly.

For instance, when I was a teenager, I remember praying to be a doctor—specifically, a heart surgeon. That's all I wanted to be from the time I was a boy right up until college. I loved science. I loved the idea of working in a big New York hospital. I loved the idea of curing people of their diseases and perhaps making new discoveries that would advance medicine. I loved daydreaming about all of this, and even though I wasn't very religious, I prayed that my dreams would come true. For a variety of reasons, I didn't achieve my goal. In fact, I never even applied to medical school. This was a big blow to me, and I was upset with God for a long time.

But was I right to be upset? Did I really want to be a surgeon? Knowing myself and my personal flaws better now, I'm sure I would have been miserably unhappy in that profession. I would have hated the long, grueling hours. I would have hated dealing with all the blood. I would have hated dealing with the hospital bureaucracy. And interacting so often with patients who had life-threatening illnesses would have exacerbated my own inclination toward cynicism and stifled all my natural feelings of empathy. In fact, I would have been forced to become a less empathetic person in order to be good at my job.

In short, when I asked God that I might be a doctor, I thought I was asking for a "fish," but I was really asking for a "snake," and, being a good Father, God refused to give it to me.

After failing to become a doctor, I switched to a different ambition. I remember praying hard to obtain a job as assistant press secretary to a local government official. I thought this position was a wonderful opportunity for me to use my writing talent to enter the world of politics. I had all kinds of dreams of running for office one day and making my mark in the world as a public figure. Maybe I'd become a congressman or a senator or even the president. Why not? But it was all going to start with this first political job. Because I knew how important the position was, I spent days and nights intently begging for God's assistance. I made all the usual, insincere promises to become a better person, to give up my sinful ways, and to go to church more often—if only God would grant me *this one little favor*.

Well, I didn't get the job, and as a result, I was even more upset with God.

Once again, however, in retrospect, I realize that a job in politics would have put me on the worst possible career path. Knowing myself, my ego, my carnality, my weaknesses, and other negative aspects of my personality, I can see I was clearly unsuited to political life. It would have led me into a world of temptations that would have been very dangerous for me, spiritually. And because of the cancel culture that has since emerged, I certainly would not have been able to hold on to the traditional Christian principles I eventually embraced and become a successful politician in a state like New York. The bottom line is, when I asked God to help me get that political job, I thought I was asking for an "egg," but I was really asking for a "scorpion." Being a good Father, God refused to give it to me.

In retrospect, then, did God really say no to my prayer? Or did He use His divine vision to look past my words and into my soul? Like my ambition to be a doctor, my ambition to be involved in politics was something I only thought I wanted. But I was mistaken. I had misread my own thoughts and feelings. Perhaps what I was really seeking was some kind of public recognition to make me feel significant; perhaps I wanted to be somebody "important"; perhaps I wanted to work in a field in which I had the opportunity to satisfy my empathetic nature by helping others.

If that's what I was praying for, then God didn't turn me down. In fact, I'm pretty sure He said yes to me. Later in this book, I'll explain why. But for now, understand this point. While it's true that God encourages us to bring our specific needs to Him in prayer—because open, honest communication often leads to a deepening relationship with Him—it's also crucial that we first attempt to understand our prayers of supplication in a less superficial way.

In other words, if you want to obtain a miracle, and you know the most important step is to ask God to give you one, you must try to dig deeper into your own consciousness before blurting out the first words that come to mind. You must try to engage in a bit more self-reflection and spiritual discernment to discover what you truly want. You must realize that your own psychology is important and that God is not going to dismiss it. Therefore, you shouldn't dismiss it either.

What is it that you desire in your heart of hearts? Think long and hard about that question. Pray long and hard about it too. I know it's not easy to come up with an answer. In fact, it's not your fault. One of the effects of Original Sin is that our intellects have been clouded over and our vision blurred. It's difficult for us to see the truth about things—especially the things of the spirit. As we grow as Christians, the theological virtue of faith, first given to us at Baptism, increases our capacity to see the world from God's perspective. But that's a long process, and even individuals who are very advanced in the spiritual life still have trouble distinguishing their spoken desires from the desires of their souls.

The important thing is to realize that there is indeed a difference. Don't accept that you want something simply because you *feel* the desire for it at this particular moment. There's a paradox at work here! What you're praying for with your tongue might be the very opposite of what you're praying for with your soul. And remember, a paradox might seem to be self-contradictory, but its purpose is to invite you to understand a deeper truth. In this case, the invitation is to understand *yourself*.

So, today, when you ask God for a miracle, try considering, in all humility, whether you might really be asking Him for stones and snakes and scorpions. If that's the case, you can't expect Him to answer you in the affirmative.

With that in mind, try incorporating the following request into what you're already praying for every day:

Lord, as I continue humbly waiting for this miracle. I ask You for the ability to discern Your will and my own will more accurately. Most importantly, aware of my own limited understanding, I ask You to look deep into my soul and give me what I truly desire.

5

Tribulation versus Courage

If you're praying for a miracle, chances are you're afraid of something.

That's nothing to be ashamed of. In fact, the biggest problem people have today is fear. We're afraid about our health. We're afraid about our finances. We're afraid about our jobs. We're afraid about our marriages. We're afraid about our kids. Most of all, we're afraid that we're not enough; that we don't have what it takes to overcome our problems; that we're not smart enough, strong enough, attractive enough, or lovable enough.

And here's where another miracle paradox comes in.

We're called to "be not afraid" and to have no anxiety, because this is a sign of our reliance on God and our belief that He can give us a peace that "transcends all understanding" (Phil. 4:7). Yet, at the same time, we're told that physical, emotional, psychological, and mental suffering can be beneficial for our spiritual growth (Rom. 5:3–5). Enduring pain—including the pain of fear—has the power to refine us like gold (1 Pet. 1:6–7) and to help us grow closer to God and understand life much more quickly and deeply than by any other method.

This apparent contradiction is a hard one to grapple with. But it's one of the most crucial if we want to obtain a miracle because it's connected so intimately with faith and trust and persistence—well-known prerequisites for miracles laid out by Christ in the Gospels.

The concept that God allows us to experience fear for our ultimate good is a deeply rooted tenet in Scripture and Christian theology. Mother Angelica, the foundress of the Eternal Word Television Network (EWTN), said, "If God sends you tribulations, He wants you to tribulate!"[14] In other words, when God permits you to experience suffering, He does so because He knows you can benefit from it. He knows He will be able to pull some greater good out of it. Mother Angelica

[14] *Mother Angelica's Little Book of Life Lessons and Everyday Spirituality*, ed. Raymond Arroyo (New York: Doubleday, 2007), 135; EWTN, *Mother Angelica Live Classics*, originally aired June 19, 1996.

herself faced numerous personal and financial challenges, including serious health issues. Each trial strengthened her resolve and her faith, fueling her to build EWTN, which reaches millions of viewers globally each day. Her suffering was not a deterrent but a catalyst for her mission.

Or take an example from Scripture. In the Second Letter to the Corinthians, we see that St. Paul was afflicted by a "thorn" in his flesh (2 Cor. 12:7). We're never told what that thorn was. It could have been a physical ailment or a temptation or an inclination to a certain kind of sin. All we know is that it was painful enough to cause St. Paul great anxiety—so much so that he begged God three times to remove the thorn. But how did God respond to St. Paul? Did He take away the pain? Did He give him some inspiring words to make the pain more bearable? No, He said: "[Enough!] My grace is sufficient for you, for my power is made perfect in weakness" (2 Cor. 12:9). After that, St. Paul wasn't afraid of his thorn anymore. In fact, he began to take pleasure in the hardships and persecutions he had to endure because he knew that somehow, in some way, God was going to help him more when he was weak and suffering and afraid than when he was feeling strong.

On a very basic level, fear can make us feel more vulnerable and less self-reliant, and therefore more dependent on

God. In fact, it's probably the very thing that motivated you to reach out to God in the first place and ask Him for a miracle. Think of a child who has had a bad dream or is afraid of a storm, or afraid of going to the doctor or the dentist, or afraid to try something new, such as learning how to swim. When that child is in the grip of fear, what's the first thing he does? Isn't it to call out to his mother or father for help? That's not the wrong thing to do—it's the right thing; it's the smart thing.

So, yes, fear can be good. It can help us to grow. It can help us to mature. It can protect us. It can focus us. It can make us sharper and keep us "on our toes," spiritually as well as emotionally and physically. It can prepare us and prune us and make us stronger. It can make us more reliant on God, which can consequently bring us closer to God. It can accomplish all these things, and it can accomplish them at an accelerated speed.

Therefore, even though it might seem counterintuitive to you—in fact, even if it goes against every fiber of your being—when God sends you fear, you should do your best to embrace it in some fashion. That doesn't mean you should *desire* it, but you should make a decisive act of the will to say to God, "I hate being afraid, but I know You wouldn't permit me to feel this way unless You knew it would also help me to grow in some way I need to grow. I know you wouldn't send me tribulations unless you wanted me to tribulate. So, thank You, Lord."

But of course, we're not done. There's the other side of the paradox we still have to deal with.

While God allows and even desires that we "tribulate" when He send us tribulations, He also commands us to pray for courage. He knows that it takes very little real terror to help us grow. He knows that there is a fine line between the benefit we can derive from fear, which is a natural, adaptive response to an immediate threat or danger; and anxiety, which is a chronic, heightened, or extended sense of worry about the future and which often causes both a physical and spiritual paralysis that can prevent us from doing God's will. Thus, from the moment God allows us to experience fear, He also desires that we immediately pray for courage to combat anxiety.

I've written about this before. In fact, I don't think there's a more important subject in the world than courage.[15] Most people don't realize it, but courage isn't needed only to confront fear—it's much, much bigger than that.

---

[15] Anthony DeStefano, *Ten Prayers God Always Says Yes To* (New York: Image, 2007); *OK, I Admit It, I'm Afraid* (Eugene,

C. S. Lewis said that courage is not merely one virtue among many but is the essential form of all virtues at their testing point. When he said this, he was echoing the assertion of Aristotle and Thomas Aquinas, who argued that for virtues to be genuinely effective, they must be applied with a resoluteness that is possible only with courage. This means that to act with honesty, mercy, chastity, magnanimity, or patience, one first needs the bravery to confront and overcome the challenges that obstruct those virtues. This is particularly important when a person is faced with strong temptations, where the true measure of courage is tested by the resolve *not to yield*.[16]

Courage is indispensable in taking any kind of constructive action or counteracting any evil. It underpins the ability to adhere to commandments, to confront physical dangers, to tackle both rational and irrational fears, and to combat neuroses and addictions. It enables perseverance

---

OR: Harvest House Publishers, 2015); *The Seed Who Was Afraid to Be Planted* (Manchester, NH: Sophia Institute Press, 2019).

[16] C. S. Lewis, *The Screwtape Letters* (New York: HarperCollins, 2001), 148; Aristotle, *Nicomachean Ethics*, trans. Martin Ostwald (Indianapolis: Bobbs-Merrill, 1962); Thomas Aquinas, *ST*, II-II, q. 123, art. 1.

through hardships, endurance of suffering, risk-taking, upholding truth, and the pursuit of any kind of ambitious endeavor. Essentially, courage is foundational to every aspect of life.

In virtually every book of the Bible, God tells us to be brave. In fact, the words "fear not," "be not afraid," or variations of that phrase appear more than a hundred times in Sacred Scripture.[17] And they aren't just suggestions—they're commands. The Bible doesn't say, "Try not to be afraid"; it says, "Don't be afraid." It doesn't say, "Do your best to be strong"; it says, "Be strong, fear not! Behold, your God will come ... and save you" (Isa. 35:4).

Why? Because God knows how scary life can be, and He also wants us to know that He gives everyone the ability to overcome the fears they face—*if they ask for it.*

Courage isn't just a skill or a talent or an ability that human beings possess. It's a gift. Yes, a person can have

---

[17] Daniel Isaiah Joseph, "How Many Times Is 'Fear Not' In the Bible?" *Christianity FAQ*, last updated July 14, 2023, https://christianityfaq.com/how-many-times-is-fear-not-in-the-bible/; Alyssa Avant, "Is 'Fear Not' Actually Written 365 Times in the Bible?" *Pray With Confidence*, last updated April 13, 2020, https://praywithconfidence.com/is-fear-not-actually-written-365-times-in-the-bible/.

a fearless disposition, in the same way that some people are born with gentle and peaceful natures. But the kind of courage we're talking about here is much more than that—it's something that is added onto our personality. Thomas Aquinas used the famous theological expression "grace builds on nature" to describe the phenomenon.[18] What this means is that God can take what we are born with, or what we have acquired in life by observation or habit, and infuse even more of it into our souls, supernaturally. Basically, He can inject us with a special divine shot of courage anytime He wants.

For instance, some individuals instinctively leap into action in perilous situations. Imagine someone spotting a building ablaze and, without hesitation, rushing in to rescue those trapped inside, disregarding the imminent dangers. Conversely, others might hesitate, weighed down by the fear of potential injury or death. Those who aren't naturally daring, however, can exhibit similar bravery if they seek divine assistance. God can "level the playing

[18] Thomas Aquinas, *ST*, I, q. 1, art. 8, ad 2; "Gratia non tollit naturam, sed perficit," Wikipedia, last edited October 4, 2023, https://en.wikipedia.org/wiki/Gratia_non_tollit _naturam,_sed_perficit.

field," empowering the naturally timid to act with as much courage as those who seem innately fearless. We've all observed the phenomenon of unassuming individuals—those who might appear frail or timid—emerging as incredible heroes. In fact, most recipients of the Congressional Medal of Honor aren't the stereotypical warriors one might expect. This fact can often be attributed to the extraordinary grace God bestows upon those who earnestly seek courage and are open to His guidance.

Remember how the apostles acted during the Passion? They deserted Christ, denied Him, and ran away from Him as far and as fast as they could. And this was after they had seen Him raise people from the dead! This was after they had seen Him walk on water, calm storms, multiply loaves and fish, exorcise demons, and perform countless miracles.

Now of course they didn't really understand what was going on, and they were afraid of being crucified themselves. But what was their excuse after the Resurrection? What was their excuse after they saw Him alive again, in His glorified body? That's when they saw Him walk through walls! They spent over a month with Him and witnessed many incredible miracles before He finally ascended into Heaven.

You would think that, after that experience, they would finally have had the courage to face their own persecution.

But did they begin preaching or healing or spreading the good news about Jesus? No. Instead, they hid in the upper room by themselves. They cloistered themselves away from everyone. They prayed and waited. It wasn't until after Pentecost, when the Holy Spirit came down upon them, that they went out and began the work of spreading the gospel.

In the final analysis, it wasn't the miracles that made the apostles fearless, nor was it hearing the message of salvation proclaimed to them or even spending time with the Lord. It was a freely bestowed gift of the Holy Spirit, *after* the apostles had prayed for it. It was only when they received courage from God in answer to prayer that they immediately left their hiding place, went outside, and began taking chances and facing danger.

Well, if they needed help from God to have the courage to carry out their mission, don't you think you do too? If you need a miracle right now, don't you think an extra dose of courage would come in handy? Don't you think that should be a special part of your prayer?

And even more importantly, praying for courage doesn't just give you a temporary boost—it sets the stage for significant growth. As with a muscle in your body, the more you use your courage, the stronger it becomes. It's possible for a person to be born with a very timid nature, afraid of his own shadow, and then, through prayer, begin receiving "infusions" of courage from God. If that courage is nurtured and exercised, then it's possible for that same timid person to become, over time, the most heroic of saints.

The problem is that this dynamic works in the opposite direction too. Just as muscles can atrophy from disuse, so can courage diminish if it's not regularly exercised. Many people neglect to seek God's strength for everyday bravery, focusing on their own willpower until they're faced with a dire crisis that demands extraordinary courage. Unfortunately, their ability to act courageously has, by then, weakened significantly. This often leads them to view life — and especially the Christian life — as overwhelmingly difficult. The reality is, they haven't been conditioning their "courage muscle" regularly, and it has left them unprepared and morally out of shape. When you desperately need a miracle, that is a bad state to be in.

I'm not saying that every challenge you encounter is due to a lack of bravery. Even those who are naturally courageous can find themselves facing severe difficulties when inherent bravery falls short. Consider all the people ensnared in self-destructive addictions. These folks, who are often kind at their core, are literally imprisoned by malevolent forces. Whether it's drugs, alcohol, gambling, or sex, battling an addiction is one of the most daunting challenges anyone can face. It consumes a person's thoughts, leaving no room for anything else, including thoughts of God. The person's energy is drained, his momentum is halted, and his hope is extinguished. Breaking free from this bondage requires immense courage—probably the greatest there is. And it's impossible to do it alone. Many attempt to, but with tragic outcomes. The result is almost always the same: sadness, despair, destruction, and sometimes death.

The same applies to various phobias, such as the fear of open spaces, or the fear of crowded or enclosed spaces, or the fear of social situations, or the fear of flying. Having one or more of these irrational fears can leave you immobilized. Overcoming them requires significant courage. It's a lengthy process, and unless you have an innate, steely resolve, it will be extremely challenging to navigate. In these instances, when you ask God for courage, He essentially tries to guide you through that process, even to the point of holding your hand as you seek, through trial and error, the right form of therapeutic help.

Along with this assistance, God grants you something else: perseverance. It takes time to conquer any addiction or phobia. There will inevitably be setbacks—methods and treatments that fail, embarrassing moments and humiliations. During these times, the natural human inclination is to feel discouraged and despondent. But if you pray for courage, you won't reach that point—in fact, you'll never lose hope. You'll receive all the bravery and strength you need to bear the cross you've been given, just as Christ bore His Cross. Thomas Aquinas considered this the highest form of courage: the ability to endure, to "bear up" against terrifying circumstances over a prolonged period.[19]

Remember my friend Fr. Brian? There was a very wealthy young woman he knew several years ago. She lived in a mansion overlooking the ocean in New Jersey. Fr. Brian had made her acquaintance when she was helping a friend of hers who was suffering from AIDS. Fr. Brian had ministered to her friend as well. But after the friend died, the young woman became very depressed and turned to drugs. In no time, she was a serious addict. Soon, all her money—which amounted to millions she had inherited from her family—was gone, and she was living on the

[19] Thomas Aquinas, *ST*, II-II, q. 137, art. 2; Msgr. Paul J. Glenn, "137. Perseverance," A Tour of the *Summa*, accessed August 27, 2024, http://www.catholictheology.info/summa-theologica/summa-part2B.php?q=161.

streets. She had literally lost every penny. That's when she showed up at Fr. Brian's rectory door. He didn't even recognize her, she was so gaunt and sickly and her clothes so ragged. She said to him: "God told me to come here. Can you help me? I'm so afraid."

Fr. Brian let her in, and they prayed together for a miracle. Then he got her into a treatment program and a halfway house. Many people in the parish who remembered the woman chipped in to help her. Slowly—very slowly—she worked to overcome her addiction. She has now been drug-free for fifteen years. Even more significantly, she is a leader in Narcotics Anonymous (NA) groups. She has helped hundreds of addicts get off the streets, beat their drug addictions, and find jobs. Helping addicts has become a ministry for her.

There are many things to learn from this story. One is that this woman's great wealth neither made her happy nor prevented her from becoming destitute. Another is that even though her whole world came crumbling down around her, her life wasn't over. In fact, it hadn't even really begun. God knew He would build her up again, this time with a different kind of wealth, one that repurposed her natural gifts and gave her life profound meaning; one that would help *Him* build up His kingdom.

The bottom line is, no matter what problem you're facing, please believe that God wants to help you. He wants you to triumph. He wants to give you "courage infusions." When you feel yourself becoming afraid of something, remember that your fear is actually a Godsend and that it can protect you, purify you, and prepare you for what's to come. But while you try to embrace this fear as a gift from God, you must also, paradoxically, ask Him to help you to transcend it so that you can take whatever action is necessary to overcome your problems. This is one of the hardest things in life to do. But when God sees you attempting it—when He sees you simultaneously welcoming His tribulation and praying to prevent its transformation into paralyzing anxiety, He *will* come to your rescue.

With that in mind, here is another petition to incorporate into your prayer for a miracle:

God, please help me to benefit and grow from the tribulation You are permitting me to endure. But also grant me the courage to triumph over my anxiety and seek whatever help I need to rise above the challenges I am facing, as I await Your miraculous intervention in my life.

6

Persistent versus Decisive Faith

Everyone knows that faith is the foundational "condition" mentioned most in the Gospels for obtaining miracles. Think of the woman hemorrhaging blood who was healed because of her faith (Mark 5:34) or the centurion whose servant was healed from a distance due to his extraordinary belief in Jesus' authority (Matt. 8:13). Jesus Himself often lamented lack of faith as a barrier to performing miracles, most notably in His hometown of Nazareth, where "he did not do many mighty works ... because of their unbelief" (Matt. 13:58).

Indeed, the primary reason Jesus performed miracles wasn't to alleviate suffering but to increase people's faith. Take the famous story in the Gospel of John in which Jesus turns water into wine. The result was that "the disciples believed in Him" (John 2:11). Obviously, the miraculous transformation wasn't just about saving a wedding celebration—it was about building faith. The Gospel further says: "Jesus performed many other signs.... These are written that you may believe that Jesus is the Messiah, the Son of God, and that by believing you may have life in his name" (John 20:30–31). Each miracle that Jesus worked was a divine invitation or "nudge," aimed at shifting people's focus from the miracle itself to God's power and love. Faith is the bridge that connects us to the divine, making the impossible possible, and with every miracle, Jesus was building that bridge.

But guess what? Faith is another one of those "conditions" that involves a paradox.

Here's what I mean. Most Christians are familiar with the biblical call to be persistent and patient in prayer. Scripture is replete with exhortations to "pray continually" (1 Thess. 5:17) and to "wait for the LORD" (Ps. 27:14).

In the Old Testament, we see Jacob, a man who "wrestles" with God until daybreak, clinging to God and refusing to let go until he finally receives a blessing (Gen. 32:24–26). Likewise, Hannah's relentless petitions for a child were eventually answered by God, and she acknowledged that it was "because I asked the LORD for him" (1 Sam. 1:20). These images of persistent, unwavering believers give us a powerful example of the kind of tenacity God wants in our prayer lives.

The New Testament abounds with this kind of encouragement. Jesus' parable of the persistent widow (Luke 18:1–8) specifically teaches that we should always pray and not give up. The widow's continual petitions to an indifferent judge ultimately lead to her receiving justice. The lesson is that if even an unjust judge can be moved by persistence, how much more will our loving God respond to His children when we reach out to Him day and night?

Likewise, Matthew 15:21–28 tells of a Canaanite woman who approaches Jesus, pleading for her daughter's healing. Even though Jesus initially ignores her, she persists with humility, acknowledging His authority by saying, "Even the dogs eat the crumbs that fall from their master's table." Her perseverance and unwavering belief lead Jesus to commend her faith and grant her request, saying, "Be it done for you as you desire" (RSVCE).

Obviously, humility and persistence are part of an effective model of all prayers of supplication. Yet, as we just saw, we are also told to pray with *decisive* faith. Mark 11:24 says: "Therefore I tell you, whatever you ask for in prayer, believe that you have received it, and it will be yours." Matthew

17:20 says: "For truly, I say to you, if you have faith as a grain of mustard seed, you will say to this mountain, 'Move from hence to yonder place,' and it will move; and nothing will be impossible to you" (RSVCE). What can this mean? On one hand, persistence in prayer suggests a continual asking, knocking, and seeking. This necessitates ongoing engagement with God, and ongoing engagement implies a kind of uncertainty. It implies that we're not sure what God is going to do, so we must try to "convince" Him. On the other hand, having a rock-solid faith implies trust that God has *already* heard us and will answer our prayers even if we utter just one with conviction.

How can these both be true? How can we be persistent—which involves uncertainty—and faithful—which involves certainty?

The answer, once again, is that this is only an apparent contradiction, a paradox that invites us to discover something deeper about our relationship with God. In this case, the persistence God requires in prayer not only tests our faith over a longer period but also makes our dependence on God more consistent. This is very important because dependence on God always equals *intimacy* with God. Therefore, in embracing both aspects of this "contradiction," our faith is refined and strengthened.

Let's talk more about faith itself. What, exactly, do we mean when we say that faith is a requirement for having miracles granted? Do we mean faith in the existence of God? Surely that can't be it. After all, the devil believes in God. The demons believe in God. There are lots of people on earth who believe in God but hate Him. And, in fact, all those folks in the Bible who received miracles took God's existence for granted; they were fervent, faithful Jews or Samaritans of first-century Palestine. Why would Jesus even ask them if they had faith in God when He already knew they did? He must have meant something else.

The faith demanded in the Gospels as a prerequisite for miracles is much more than simple belief in the "existence of God" or even belief that Jesus *is* God. It has to do with believing in God's *power and desire* to perform miraculous things for us, *through* Jesus.

Yes, we may believe that God created the world and everything in it and that Jesus is His Son, but does this same God really, truly care about us? Does He know us, individually? Is He just a God who observes us "from a distance," as the old song says, or is He right here with us now, profoundly interested in our welfare, intimately involved in our lives, and concerned with even the tiniest details? And most importantly, is He willing to help us in a practical way with the problems we are having, to jump-start or deepen our relationship with Him?

That's the kind of faith that Jesus is looking for—one that's focused on building a relationship with Him.

I said at the outset of this book that I haven't experienced any big aha moments in my life. That's true, but like everyone else, I do have plenty of stories of strange coincidences that, in retrospect, seem to have resulted from the hand of God. Years ago, after I first became committed to my faith again, I went through a period of spiritual turmoil in which I wondered if God was listening to my prayers. I couldn't overcome some nagging sins—one of which was my Neapolitan-Sicilian temper. There were other difficulties too, and I would often pray for guidance and help. Yet nobody "up there" seemed to hear or care enough to answer me. I felt frustrated and almost in despair.

One night, I took my six-year-old nephew to a baseball game. It was his first time in a major league ballpark, and he was naturally excited by all the sights and sounds. Most of all, he was excited by the possibility of catching a foul ball. He even brought his little baseball glove and wore it throughout the game, holding it up in anticipation before every pitch. Of course, I felt sorry for him. What chance did he have to catch a ball in a stadium full of people? As the game progressed, the home team started losing badly, and many of the fans began to leave. I wanted to leave too (impatience being one of the problems God hadn't helped me with), but my nephew wanted to stay till the very end. Finally, in the ninth inning, when the last batter was at the plate, I remember standing up when two strikes had been called and stepping over into the aisle in preparation for leaving. I also remember saying a quick prayer to God: "Lord, I know it's not important, but if You're listening now, can You please send us a foul ball—not for me but for this poor, innocent kid?" The prayer was uttered in silence, and as God is my witness, the instant the words had left my mind, the batter hit a screaming line drive to the exact spot where I had been sitting a second before; the ball bounced off the back of the seat directly into my hands, and without thinking or hesitating, I immediately plopped it into my nephew's glove. He jumped up, held the ball over his head triumphantly and started screaming with joy, and everyone around us began applauding. All of this took place before I even realized what had happened.

Now, I do not relate this as a miracle story. I know many of you reading this book have real problems and need real miracles to solve them. I don't want to trivialize those problems by telling you that God gave me a baseball. But I will say that the speed and precision with which my prayer was answered has always stuck in my head. I had been struggling with these very questions: Can God hear me? If so, is He listening? Does He care in the slightest about my requests? Will He ever answer me? And after all my doubting, here was what seemed to be a clear answer. That line drive—like a bullet fired directly at me, and one that I saw coming in both slow motion and in a flash—from the moment I uttered my prayer to the crack of the bat to the whiz of the ball to its pop off the seat into my hands and into my nephew's glove—and all of it unexpected—had the effect of stopping me from whining and complaining to God any further.

I realized that He hadn't really performed this little "miracle" for my nephew. Rather, He had performed it for me. Knowing my struggles (and now in hindsight, knowing that I would one day write a book about miracles), He wanted to show me that, yes, He absolutely was listening to every word I prayed and that He had the power to answer me with surgical precision and incredible speed. The only reason He hadn't up till then was that He didn't want to magically solve my problems. Instead, He wanted me to keep struggling for the good of my soul. Indeed, His refusal had nothing do with a lack of power or willingness;

it had to do with the fact that I needed to grow more in my relationship with Him—and He was graciously giving me a nudge in that direction.

Another thing I learned from this incident was that all my impassioned pleas had accomplished less than this simple, silent request I had made on someone else's behalf, almost without thinking. Yes, God had certainly heard my emotional prayers, but it was this calm, detached one that He chose to use to dispel my doubts.

And here we come to a significant problem we need to discuss: confusing genuine faith with emotionalism.

Some people think that if they can just *feel* strongly enough, it will convince God to grant their prayers. This is what the Evangelical congregation I mentioned a few chapters back did when that six-year-old girl became sick. It's what I did when my father was ill. We all tried hard to whip ourselves into a spiritual-emotional fervor, believing that intense feelings equated to faith that could "move mountains." But unfortunately, despite our sincerity, we didn't receive the healing miracles we so desperately sought.

In fact, when you think about it, emotionalism didn't help Our Lord either. In the Garden of Gethsemane, Jesus was so overcome with fear and anguish that He sweat drops of blood. His reaction wasn't wrong. Quite the contrary. It was a natural response to the prospect of being tortured to death. It makes perfect sense that He felt afraid and that His human nature would recoil at the idea of pain. That's one of the reasons He prayed to His Father to "remove this cup" if possible (see Luke 22:42).

But His Father didn't remove it.

The point here is not to say that Jesus should have suppressed His emotions during His agony in the garden or that the Evangelical congregation and I should have stifled our feelings when we were pleading with God for a miracle. The point is that the emotions we exhibited were completely *irrelevant* to the granting of our requests. They had nothing to do with the definition of true faith; and they did not—in these instances at least—influence God's response.

Please don't mistake my meaning. There's absolutely nothing wrong with getting emotional about your faith. There's a place for weeping and wailing with sorrow and a place for shouting and singing for joy. In fact, if you're truly in love with the Lord, then of course there will be times when you are caught up with powerful feelings. When King David was in the presence of the Ark—which contained the tablets on which God had written the Ten Commandments—he "danced before the LORD with all his might" (2 Sam. 6:14–22). That was a natural reaction for someone who understood the truth about God. So I'm not criticizing anyone who is "on fire" for the gospel. And I have nothing but admiration for my brother and sister Christians who are more demonstrative in their faith than most of the lackluster, lukewarm, la-di-da Catholics I see falling asleep at Mass half the time. All I'm saying is that emotionalism in general — no matter how sincere — doesn't do very much to "move" God. He understands that human beings blow hot and cold from minute to minute. Thus, when it comes to performing miracles, He's just not that influenced by outward displays of feeling. He's more interested in something else — something deeper.

And this is the vital lesson of this chapter: the faith required for miracles is not measured by emotional intensity but by the steadfastness and persistence of a person's *decision* to trust in God. In fact, faith is not a feeling at all. Like trust, forgiveness, and love, it is an act of the will. I've talked about this in multiple books, but it bears repeating.[20] People today are so confused about feelings. Feelings

[20] For a similar treatment of this subject, see Anthony DeStefano, *30 Days to Your New Life: A Guide to Transforming Yourself from Head to Soul* (Manchester, NH: Sophia Institute Press, 2023), chap. 15, "Time to Get Off the Fence."

are *not* steadfast. Feelings are *not* persistent. Feelings are *not* decisive. On the contrary, feelings are inconsistent, deceptive, and unreliable.

They are also notoriously fickle. One moment, you might feel utterly despondent; the next, you could be on top of the world. Your emotions can swing from gloom to joy without warning. Various factors, such as your diet, the weather, a piece of music, or the company you keep, can dramatically alter your mood. Often, you might not even understand why your emotions have shifted. Feelings can be joyful, passionate, somber, or restless. The one thing they never seem to be is predictable.

Don't underestimate the devil's grasp of this phenomenon. He's very adept at exploiting our feelings. Indeed, one of his most effective strategies is to convince us to act based on our emotions rather than on reasoned decisions. By doing this, he aims to draw us away from our higher nature. Remember, human beings are made in the "image and likeness of God," which means that we possess an intellect and free will.[21] This is something akin to God's essence. It's what sets us apart from the rest of creation.

[21] See Gen. 1:26; *Catechism of the Catholic Church* (CCC), nos. 1701, 1705.

It's what enables us to "mirror" the Trinitarian glory of God in our lives. This is such a crucial point: decisions of faith stem from our Godlike attributes—our intellect and our free will. In contrast, our emotions do not "mirror" God—at least not directly. They arise much more from our bodies.

This is not to say that emotions are bad. Far from it. They, too, are creations of God and originate in Him. God is not a cold or computer-like Being. He is the very embodiment of joy (something very different from pleasure). But just because emotions were created by God, that doesn't mean they reflect His image in the same way that our intellect and free will do. Human emotions, though rooted in our God-given souls, are primarily physiological in nature and are manifested biologically through our brains, nervous systems, sensory-motor systems, and other bodily components. Consequently, they do not resemble the image of God's essence and, in theological terms, are considered to be our "lower faculties."[22]

[22] Thomas Aquinas, *ST*, I, q. 20, art. 1, I, q. 81, art. 3; Rob Lister, *God Is Impassible and Impassioned: Toward a Theology of Divine Emotion* (Wheaton, IL: Crossway, 2012), 108–121; CCC 1763–1765; "Does God Have Emotions?"

Thus, you can't afford to be misled by them. Relying on your emotions to guide your faith is a path to deception and destruction. Remember, emotions can fluctuate wildly—like a roller coaster—propelling you from highs to lows and back, driving you to extremes. This instability makes it difficult to prevail in any kind of spiritual endeavor, much less "convince" God to give you a miraculous gift. The simple reason is that emotions can obscure, confuse, and cloud the persistent faith the Bible says you need in order to be receptive to miracles. In fact, you can't persist in anything if you're ruled by your feelings. Thus, your feelings can sometimes even be said to be in *opposition* to faith. I know this runs counter to what many spiritual people believe, but it's true. Persistent faith must be able to survive your mood!

What does "persistent faith" look like? I'll tell you. It's quiet. It's calm. It's controlled. Yes, it's a decision that can be repeated and continually assented to. But at its core, it's not emotional—at least, it doesn't have to be. Here's an example: Every morning, millions of people get up and drive to work. During their commute, only a

---

Got Questions, accessed August 27, 2024, https://www.gotquestions.org/does-God-have-emotions.html.

thin yellow line separates them from oncoming traffic. They pass all kinds of cars and trucks and trailers that are going more than sixty miles an hour and headed straight toward them. They don't know the drivers of those vehicles. They have no clue what their driving records are or whether any of them has a drinking problem. If just one of those other drivers swerved a few feet, a crash would occur. Yet these commuters go steadfastly along without blinking an eye as hundreds of vehicles whiz past them. And they do it every day. How? The reason is they've made a calm, rational decision to have faith that those other drivers will stick to their side of the road, and they are persistent in that decision. They don't "change their mind" about it.

At home, it's the same story. Right now, you might be reading this book in your living room or your home office or your bedroom. Above you is a ceiling. Have you ever inspected it? Have you checked to see if the support beams are nailed in properly or if the wood has been eaten away by termites? When was the last time you verified that all the building permits were in order? For all you know, the whole structure might suddenly collapse and crush you. And yet are you nervous at all? Is your heartbeat racing any faster? Is your blood pressure raised?

Why not? Because you've made a decision, perhaps unconsciously, to have faith that the people who built your house were professionals who did everything they were supposed to do to make sure your home environment was safe.

Understand, I'm not comparing oncoming traffic or your bedroom ceiling to the miracles Christ performed in the Gospels. I'm saying that the faith required to obtain a miracle is more like the normal, self-forgetful faith you use to live rationally in the world and go about your daily routine than it is like the passionate hallelujahs you sometimes hear in church or the sobbing supplications to God that people make to spare them from this or that calamity.

Yes, in praying for a miracle, you might not be able to quell your anxious feelings, but they're not going to help you obtain what you want. In fact, they might even hinder you because all that turmoil might paralyze your intellect and free will, thereby keeping you from making a calm, firm, sure decision to believe in God's power and His willingness to help you.

When my friend Fr. Brian was a young priest, he gave a presentation on prayer at a communion breakfast. Afterward, he sat down at his table to eat, and a woman who was suffering from debilitating multiple sclerosis (MS) went over to him slowly, struggling to walk with her cane. She asked him to pray over her. He said he'd be glad to make an appointment to see her and pulled out his calendar to set a date. But the woman held her hand up and said, "No, right now. Can you please pray over me right now?" Fr. Brian naturally felt a little uncomfortable praying over someone in the middle of a noisy dining room, but he made a quick decision to step outside his comfort zone and oblige her. Standing up, he quietly started to pray. Some of the people around him noticed he was praying and stopped their talking to look. More people noticed, and soon a hushed silence had fallen over the whole room. Even though no one said a word, Fr. Brian could sense that many others were silently praying with him.

A few days after the communion breakfast, the woman's MS symptoms vanished. Her disease had gone into complete remission.

That was thirty years ago. In that time, the woman has lived a very normal life and can still walk and talk and even dance occasionally. For three decades, her symptoms have not progressed. Doctors will tell you that that kind of prolonged remission of MS is very rare.

My point in relating this story is that when God wants to perform a miracle, He doesn't need to see you working yourself up into a spiritual-emotional frenzy. He doesn't need "proof" that you have faith. Sometimes a simple, quick, quiet prayer, said in the middle of a crowded room, with boldness and sincerity, is all you need to produce extraordinary results.

The truth is that when it comes to obtaining a miracle, how faithful you feel doesn't matter that much. In the Gospel, there's a story about a man in the crowd who begged Jesus to heal his son. The boy had been suffering from some kind of demonic illness since childhood, and no one could cure him. But Jesus assured the boy's father, "All things are possible to him who believes." The father famously responded, "I believe; help my unbelief!" (Mark 9:23-24, RSVCE).

This perfectly illustrates the point I've been trying to make. Without any hesitation, the father made a decision: "I believe." But then he followed it up with an emotional plea: "Help my unbelief." He was basically saying that even though he had decided to believe, there was still a part of him that didn't *feel* certitude.

But what did Jesus do? Did He criticize the man? Did He tell him he needed more faith? Did He say he had to feel more deeply? No! He immediately reached out and healed the man's son. In other words, the father's decision to believe was enough. It was all that Jesus required to grant his request and show him the healing power of God.

The same goes for you and me.

If you really want a miracle and you've been following the advice in this book so far, the next thing you should do is try to avoid being so flustered and frustrated! Even if your whole body is trembling, do your best to pause, recollect yourself, and put aside your emotions. Stop the moaning. Stop the crying. Stop the pleading. Stop the pacing. Stop the talking. Stop the worrying about all the terrible things that might happen if you *don't* get your miracle.

Just decide, in the same way that you've decided to drive your car in the morning or sit in a room of your home under a ceiling, to believe the Lord is listening to your prayers and has the power and willingness to help you. Period.

And if you're on the other end of the emotional spectrum, and you love Jesus with all your heart and soul, stop trying to *feel* grateful and elated and gloriously enraptured that He is going to give you your miracle. Yes, you can calmly thank Him for hearing you. Yes, if you have been given the grace and consolation of being joyful during your suffering, of course you can express your appreciation and share your optimism with others. But in terms of obtaining the miracle you want, there's no need for any great fanfare—either negative or positive.

For at least the time it takes to pray, do your best just to sit there quietly and get in touch with your intellect and free will—those parts of your soul made in the image and likeness of God. Don't try to feel certitude. *Think* certitude. Use your intellect and free will right now to make a simple faith choice. Take a few minutes to embody the words of Psalm 46:10:

Be still and know that I am God.

Then you can add the following request to the prayer you've been saying:

Lord, please give me the persistence and the perseverance to continue entreating Your aid, even if my petition is not immediately answered. At the same time, give me the resolve to make a definitive faith decision to believe in Your power and willingness to provide what is necessary for the good of my soul.

Say this prayer in the same calm way later tonight. And tomorrow morning. And tomorrow night. And the following day. Say it regularly. Show God you're not going to change your mind if you don't get your miracle right away. Do this with as much dedication as Jacob and Hannah and the old widow in the Gospel.

If you keep it up, day after day, night after night, peacefully "waiting on the Lord," then be assured you *do* have faith as large as a mustard seed, and it *is* enough to move mountains.

7

Self-Reliance versus Surrender to God

The words "faith" and "trust" are often used interchangeably. Indeed, they're closely related, theologically. But they can have different meanings. In the context of biblical miracles, "faith" often refers to belief in God's power and promises, while "trust" implies a *personal reliance* on God and *surrender* to His providential care. This is an important distinction because Jesus seems to impose both "conditions" when He performs many of His miracles.

For example, in Mark 5:34, Jesus says to the woman who touched His cloak, "Daughter, your faith has healed you. Go in peace and be freed from your suffering." Here, faith signifies belief in Jesus' power to heal. In Mark 4:40, however, we see Jesus reprimanding His disciples after calming the stormy sea: "Why are you so afraid? Do you still have no faith?" Here He is emphasizing the need for trust in God's providence even in dangerous situations.

In the last chapter, we talked about the need to have a calm, steadfast, decisive faith in God's ability and willingness to perform miracles. Now we turn to the second condition of "faith": trusting that God wants to help us with the problems we are facing and, more importantly, surrendering to His will because we know that no matter how those problems eventually turn out, God will somehow pull a greater good out of them.

This can be a difficult subject to discuss. To live is to suffer—sometimes to suffer intensely. And when intense suffering comes and you have no choice but to beg God for a miracle, the only thing that can really help is to abandon yourself totally to His divine will.

I wrote about this kind of surrender in a book called *30 Days to Your New Life: A Guide to Transforming Yourself from Head to Soul.* I'm going to quote from that book at length now because if you're really going through significant pain, I think you need to hear these words.[23] If you're not suffering intensely, you can skip this chapter. But since

---

[23] DeStefano, *30 Days to Your New Life*, chap. 26, "Intense Suffering."

everyone at some point goes through the fire of torment and misery, you might want to at least glance at it.

What you first must understand is that nothing happens in the universe unless God either wills it or permits it to happen. Nothing happens to *you* unless God wills it or permits it to happen. Nothing in life occurs by chance; nothing is an accident; nothing is a coincidence. This is the providence or "divine plan" of God.

I'm not trying to say here that the suffering we experience in life—cancer, heart disease, financial ruin, poverty, death, and so on—is something God likes. God is not a sadistic puppeteer dangling human beings over a hot fire for His amusement. These terrible things entered the world because of a choice that Adam and Eve freely made in the Garden of Eden. God hates suffering as much as we do. He mourns *with* us when we are experiencing agony. He is just like any father who feels bad when his children fall and hurt themselves. But God allows our suffering because He created a world in which free will prevails, and—because of that—pain and evil and suffering exist.

In other words, God doesn't cause suffering. But He permits it.

Believe it or not, that kind of world is actually better in the long run. It makes a deeper, more profound kind of happiness possible because it's predicated on freedom and not on automation. As we've noted, anything that's programmed can't be happy. Essentially, God permits evil only because He knows that someday, by the mysterious workings of His divine providence, He's going to pull some greater good out of it.

What possible greater good might come out of your present hardship?

Maybe it will bring you closer to God; after all, I said in the last chapter that dependence on God equals intimacy with Him. Or maybe this is a chance for you to grow more knowledgeable and empathetic and help others who have the same problem. Or maybe this is an opportunity for you to receive help from other people and become humbler. All we can say for sure is that whenever God allows you to undergo a period of trial, He's trying to purify you; He's trying to "prune the vine." And the goal of every purification and every pruning is always the same: to produce more fruit. God wants you to produce more fruit for Him and for His Kingdom. And though you may not realize it when you're experiencing pain, more fruit always means more *life*. When God gives you suffering, He is actually giving you the opportunity to do more and to grow more and to love more and therefore to live more.

That's why you have to accept on faith that everything in life—whether it's wealth, poverty, sickness, health, blessings, or trials—comes from the hand of God and ultimately is for the benefit of your immortal soul.

Now, it's important to be careful here. Trust in God's providential will isn't to be confused with fatalism. It doesn't rob you of your free will and your obligation to act in a morally responsible way. It doesn't lead to laziness or procrastination or cowardice. Just because God is in charge, that doesn't mean that you can sit back and do nothing when action is called for. Quite the contrary. If a problem arises, you have to deal with it. If you're sick, you have to call a doctor. If you're in legal trouble, you have to call a lawyer. If you're in a financial hole, you have to climb your way out of it. If you see an injustice, you have to fight it. God expects you to do everything that needs to be done to solve your problem. In fact, the very act of praying for a miracle often leads to the kind of action that will help bring about something "miraculous"; for example, it can lead you to the right hospital, the right doctor, the right banker, the right teacher, the right friend, or the priest or counselor or stranger who can help you.

And that brings us to the next miracle paradox: if you want a miracle, you are called to trust God by surrendering yourself to His will, believing that He knows what is best for you. This requires humility and acceptance of your limitations, acknowledging that you are not in control of life. At the same time, God also wants you to be self-reliant, to do everything the situation calls for, and to make use of all your God-given talents. As St. Augustine famously said of this paradox, "Pray as though everything depended on God. Work as though everything depended on you."[24]

Most people who are under great pressure have no choice but to fulfill the second part of this equation. They're already in a crisis mode and must act. But the first part of the paradox is equally important. You must be able to let go and relinquish. After you do whatever you're supposed to do, you must try your best to be at peace, to know in the deepest part of your soul that God is in charge. If, despite your best efforts, all your hopes and dreams seem to be dashed, you have to accept that as part of God's plan for you.

[24] See Jim Manney, "Work as if Everything Depends on God," IgnatianSpirituality.com, accessed August 27, 2024, https://www.ignatianspirituality.com/work-as-if-everything-depends-on-god/.

That's not easy to do. As we said earlier, it's sometimes impossible to control your feelings, even on an hour-to-hour basis. If you have a chronic problem with anxiety or panic attacks, it's even more challenging. Of course, there are breathing techniques and self-help strategies you can find online, and if the problem is serious enough, there are medications that can help you. But if you're like most people, and you're only going through a temporary bout of stress and fear because of a specific problem in your life, the most important thing you can do is get control of your will and place yourself in God's hands.

Trusting God, like having faith in God, isn't about feelings. It's about willpower. When you see yourself worrying about a problem, when you see the anxiety and fear starting to build inside you, that's the time to make a conscious effort to take a breath, recollect yourself, and say with confidence, "I know You're here with me, Lord. I know You're watching over me. I know this is Your will. I know that nothing happens without Your permission."

So, while your emotions may revolt and even tremble, your will can still be at peace and say, "No, I will not be afraid."

Let's be honest. Everyone's life is in question every day. There is absolutely no certainty about life or death. At any moment, you can have a heart attack or a brain aneurysm; you can be in a car accident or get hit by a bus. The same God who gave you the morning does not promise you the evening. Each day is truly and literally a gift. Whenever God allows you to get a serious illness or face any kind of problem (even if the problem is something you brought on yourself), He wants to make that point clear. He wants to drive home the fact that everyone's life is in His hands, that everyone must literally depend on Him for every breath they take.

Think of all the factors that had to be in place for you even to come into existence. Think of all the things that could have gone wrong when you were conceived or while you were in the womb. Think of all the things that have gone wrong in your life up till now. Think of all the situations God has brought you through safely. Think of all that He has arranged and taken care of in your life. Think of all the big prayers He has answered.

That same God who has cared for you throughout your life is going to take care of you today, tomorrow, and every other day. If you're trying your best to trust Him, either He will shield you from suffering, or He will give you the strength to bear it.

Remember, the devil delights in your fear and anxiety. Anxiety is the greatest spiritual enemy, after sin. Why?

Because anxiety is like addictions and phobias. It incapacitates you. It paralyzes you. St. Francis de Sales compared anxiety to a cold winter day that descends on the forest and causes all the animals to hide and causes the trees not to grow. That's what anxiety does to us—it brings winter to our souls, so we can't do the will of God. And that's why, at every Catholic Mass, the priest says:

> Deliver us, Lord,... from every evil, graciously grant peace in our days, that, by the help of your mercy, we may be always free from sin and safe from all distress.[25]

Stress takes so much of our energy and time that can be used for better things—such as helping others, loving others, and sacrificing for others. It stops all goodness and leaves a void in which the devil has space to operate to the maximum extent. There's an old saying: "The devil fishes in troubled waters."[26] If you are stressed and need

---

[25] *The Roman Missal*, 3rd typical ed. (Washington, DC: United States Conference of Catholic Bishops, 2011), 127.

[26] St. Francis de Sales, *Introduction to the Devout Life*, trans. and ed. John K. Ryan (New York: Image Books, 1989), pt. 4, chap. 11.

a miracle, you must not allow him to do that because it can prevent you from receiving your miracle.

Of course, there may be times when it seems impossible for you to be at peace; times when you're deathly afraid that something terrible might happen, such as financial ruin, or the breakup of your marriage, or cancer; times when you literally find it difficult to breathe, when your whole body goes limp, when your knees start to buckle and the only thing you want to do is collapse somewhere—anywhere—and close your eyes and shut out the whole world.

In such dark days of radical fear, radical surrender to God is the only answer. Christ says in the Gospel, "Fear is useless; what is needed is trust" (see Mark 5:36). The simple fact is that the more you trust God, the more He'll help you get through whatever crisis you're experiencing. No matter how great your fear, you must keep saying, with St. Faustina, "Jesus, I trust in You; Jesus, I trust in You." It doesn't matter if you repeat this holy exclamation a million times. Just keep saying it over and over again, out loud and to yourself, morning, noon, and night, as you drift off to sleep and as you wake up. You must try to make it part of your very being.

Now, what does the paradox of "surrendering in trust to Jesus" while being "self-reliant" look like, in practical terms?

It means going about your daily work *without thinking about the problem you have left in Jesus' hands*. If you have a job, and you're physically able, you should keep on working. If there are meetings you have to attend, attend them. If you have projects you have to complete, complete them. If there's a certain exercise routine you're supposed to follow, follow it. If there's a certain medical examination you have to take, take it. There's a quote attributed to Winston Churchill that sums up this principle perfectly: "When you're going through hell, the best thing to do is *keep going*."[27]

The way you show God that you trust Him is by soldiering through and not letting your problems consume all your thoughts and emotions and activities. Essentially, you show your trust in God by forcing yourself *not* to think about your problems but, instead, letting *Him* think about them.

Another important point to keep in mind has to do with timing. Christ said, "Do not be anxious about tomorrow,

[27] "If You're Going through Hell, Keep Going," Quote Investigator, September 14, 2014, https://quoteinvestigator .com/2016/01/29/keep-going/; Michael Richards, "Red Herrings: Famous Quotes Churchill Never Said," International Churchill Society, June 9, 2013, https://winston churchill.org/publications/finest-hour/finest-hour-141 /red-herrings-famous-quotes-churchill-never-said/.

for tomorrow will be anxious for itself. Let the day's own trouble be sufficient for the day" (Matt. 6:34, RSVCE). What that means is that God gives you divine assistance, or *grace*, only for the present day; and He dispenses that grace only one day at a time. He doesn't give you grace for tomorrow or for next week or for next month. Just for this one twenty-four-hour period. That's why the fear of some future suffering is always greater than the suffering itself. When you're thinking about painful events that might take place tomorrow, you are not yet being given the grace God intends to give you at the moment you'll be experiencing those events. This is a key point to grasp. The pain you have now in anticipating your suffering is greater than the actual suffering will be, because right now you're not being given any divine help to deal with that suffering. You're only being given help to get through the day.

What that means is that when you undergo any kind of great fear and anxiety, one of the most important things you must do is *shorten your time frame*. You need to focus specifically and exclusively on the one day that you're presently living. You can't keep repeating all the various nightmare scenarios in your head. You can't think about the financial ruin you might experience next week, or the scandal you might be involved in two weeks from now, or the cancer that might possibly spread next month, or the complications that might occur during surgery in two months, or the person you love dying next year. All that worrying about future disasters is useless. As I said in the last chapter about emotionalism in general, it can be an obstacle to receiving divine help from God.

Yes, an obstacle. God wants you to trust Him. And thinking about all those terrible things that aren't even necessarily going to happen is not a sign of trust. It's a sign of presumption and despair and faithlessness. God is interested in giving you divine assistance only today and only if you trust Him. If you welcome that assistance, He is going to help you *solve* your problems tomorrow.

Therefore, if you're anxiety-ridden and need a miracle, your goal is not to think about the coming days and weeks and months. Your goal is to get through the day. You *must* get through the day and make it to nighttime. That's your main objective in life whenever you experience crippling anxiety. And when you finally get to bed, sleep is your reward.

Don't underestimate the power of sleep. Sleep is powerful. Sleep is your friend. Two things happen when you sleep. One is spiritual: the Bible says that God pours out His blessings on those He loves when they slumber (see

Ps. 127:2); that's because they are trusting Him with their problems. The other is physical: the body does all its internal repair work at night; all your systems go into a "sleep mode" and actually work on fixing themselves. So, if you're experiencing profound stress, your objective is always to get a good night's sleep.

Though I'm not a physician, and though I normally don't give medical advice in my books on spirituality, it is my firm opinion that if you need help sleeping, you shouldn't hesitate to buy an over-the-counter sleep aid or ask your doctor to prescribe something stronger. Listen, it's neither silly nor cowardly to knock yourself out if you have to! Do whatever is necessary at night to sleep soundly. Your bedroom should be a safe haven for you, not a torture chamber of horrors. Once you're there—once you've made it through the day, you have to be able to put your troubles aside. You have to be able to place whatever "cross" God has given you in the corner, against the wall; then climb into bed, give all your anxiety to God, go to sleep, and let *Him* work on your problems for the next eight hours—as well as let your body heal itself and build up your energy reserves so you can do all you need to do the *following* day.

Don't worry about your cross—it will still be there when you get up.

Remember the miracle of Jesus walking on the water (Matt. 14:22–33)? As the disciples battled a fierce storm on the Sea of Galilee, Jesus came to them, in the middle of the night. When Peter saw the Lord, he asked if he could go to Him. In other words, he asked for the miracle of being able to walk on water too. Jesus said yes, and Peter stepped out of the boat and began walking.

Understand that *every step* Peter took was supported by a miracle. And every miracle was the result of Peter's trust in Jesus. But when Peter took his eyes off the Lord, focusing instead on the wind and the waves, he immediately began to sink. It's encouraging for us to know that the Lord didn't let Peter perish. Instead, He reached out and saved him. Neither does God permit us to perish every time we fail to trust Him. He's patient with us and doesn't let us drown because we sometimes doubt Him.

The point is that when we pray for a miracle, every day is like a step Peter took on the water, and every day God will provide for us if we trust Him. Indeed, sometimes God will grant us a miracle only in this way, one day at a time.

If you're going through a serious problem, I assure you that you have the power to radically surrender to God in this manner. As St. Paul says, you must "dismiss all anxiety from your mind" (see Phil. 4:6). That isn't a suggestion of his. It is a command from God. And God would not command us to do something unless He also gave us the power to follow that command. Think of a judge in a courtroom. When he slams the gavel down in front of him, it means no more questions, no more witnesses, no more cross-examinations, case dismissed! That's what you must do when you find that your mind keeps coming back and circling around the same fearful thoughts. You must bang the gavel down and say, "Enough! Stop! Case dismissed!"

So, to recap this miracle paradox, when you're going through anxiety or grieving, you should do everything you're supposed to do but, at the same time, make a decision to surrender to God's will. Keep your time frame short. Get through the day. Say over and over, "Jesus, I trust in You." Do your best to carry on with all your normal activities, not to fixate on your problems, and to strive to be even more fruitful, more helpful, and more loving to those around you. If the world and all its troubles are overwhelming you, read over these words of Jesus and put your trust in them:

> I have told you these things, so that in me you may have peace. In this world you will have trouble.

But take heart! I have overcome the world. (John 16:33)

Finally, add the following request to the prayer you are saying every day:

Lord, as I pray for this miracle, help me to fulfill all my duties and take whatever actions are necessary to address the challenges I face. But even as I diligently carry out my responsibilities, help me to trust in Your divine will and to abandon and surrender myself to it.

8

Dying to Yourself versus
Living Your Best Self

G. K. Chesterton said that the most incredible thing about miracles is that they happen.[28]

The question is: Why do they happen? To answer this, we need to go back to the beginning and try to understand why God created everything in the first place. Once we grasp that, the rest will fall into place.

God created the universe and the angels and human beings for one reason: to share the joy He has had from all eternity (CCC 293–294). "God is love" (1 John 4:8), and the essence of love is to go outside oneself and give to

[28] G. K. Chesterton, "The Blue Cross," in *The Collected Works of G. K. Chesterton*, vol. 12, *The Father Brown Stories* (San Francisco: Ignatius Press, 1990), 82.

others. Even though God is a Trinity—Father, Son, and Holy Spirit—and even though He is perfectly happy being a "family of three" and a "unity of one," He nevertheless wanted to give His happiness to other beings—so He created them. That's the reason we're here, and no other.

Now, as I've said several times, to be truly happy you can't be programmed; you must have free will. The problem is that if you have free will and the capacity to be happy, you also have the choice to go against God. And if God is love, truth, goodness, beauty, and joy, and you go contrary to Him, the result is that you'll be immersed in those qualities that are opposite to God: loneliness, lies, evil, ugliness, and misery.

God doesn't want that to happen, so He has gone out of His way to help us make the right choice, to point us in the correct direction. The most obvious of His "pointers" is the miracle of creation. Romans 1:20 says: "For ever since the world was created, people have seen the earth and sky. Through everything God made, they can clearly see His invisible qualities—His eternal power and divine nature. So they have no excuse for not knowing God."

In other words, because of the miracle of creation and life, we should be so grateful to God that we desire to do His will and avoid going against Him. Yet, despite the fact that we can "clearly see" God's invisible qualities from the world around us, it seems that we're *so* familiar with the world that we *don't* marvel at it. Quite the reverse: we take it for granted. And the more we learn about science and the intricacies of life, the less wonder we feel. Theoretical processes such as evolution—because of their slow and gradual nature—fool us into thinking that life is *not* a miracle. They make us even more indifferent to creation—as if a slow miracle were any less astonishing than a fast miracle! As Chesterton said, the real question we should be asking is not "What speed are things happening?" but "Why does anything happen at all?"[29]

So, what does God do when He sees this abiding and abysmal apathy in the face of His awe-inspiring creation? He has many options, but two stand out as the most efficacious. First, He can break us out of our world-weariness by sending us trials. After all, the threat of deprivation is always sure to make us more appreciative of what we have. Another option He has is to perform miracles. Indeed, one of the purposes of smaller, targeted miracles is to point out the more magnificent miracle of creation

[29] Chesterton, *Orthodoxy*, 62.

itself. As Chesterton noted, "The whole order of things is as outrageous as any miracle which could presume to violate it."[30] C. S. Lewis put it this way: "Miracles are a retelling in small letters of the very same story which is written across the whole world in letters too large for some of us to see."[31]

Basically, God uses miracles—which appear to us to be shocking exceptions to the rule—to jolt us awake. The "big picture" of creation is apparently too far away for us to be impressed by it, or too slow moving for us to notice it at all. By inserting an abrupt change into the process—one that happens close to home and affects our lives in a dramatic way—God is able to startle us into realizing that creation originated not from a collection of invisible and unthinking "laws of science" but, rather, from the purposeful will of a Creator.

Once our amazement and gratitude have been roused, we can begin moving in the right direction. And the sooner we start doing that, the sooner our faith will increase, the sooner we will change our sinful ways, and the sooner

---

[30] Chesterton, *Orthodoxy*, 154.

[31] C. S. Lewis, *God in the Dock: Essays on Theology and Ethics* (Grand Rapids: Wm. B. Eerdmans, 1970), 29.

we'll be able to experience the kind of joy that God has wanted to share with us from the beginning—right here on earth and later on in Heaven.

Do you see the connection between creation and miracles? They have not only the same point of origin—God— but also the same reason for being: to help us freely choose God and come into closer union with Him. If you are reading this book right now and need a miracle, I hope you understand that there is no point whatsoever in praying for one if that's not the result you want too!

This brings us to the next miracle paradox—and, in some ways, the paradox of all paradoxes: if you want to gain your life, you must first lose it; if you want to live, you must first die to yourself (Matt. 16:25; John 3:3-7; John 12:24).

What can these mysterious words mean?

I can tell you that they mainly have to do with the concept of *transformation*. When we think of Jesus' miracles, our minds automatically jump to the dramatic healings—the blind given sight, the lepers cleansed, the paralyzed given the power to walk. But when we dig deeper, we see that these miracles always came with a call to a radical moral transformation, to a 180-degree change of heart.

Remember the famous healing of the paralytic in Capernaum. When friends of the crippled man went to great lengths to lower him through a roof to reach Jesus, the first thing Jesus said to the cripple was, "Son, your sins are forgiven" (Mark 2:5). This was startling to the onlookers. They expected a physical healing first, but Jesus was concerned with the man's spiritual state. *That* was what was paramount to Him. Only after addressing the man's sin did Jesus say, "I say to you, rise, take up your pallet and go home" (Mark 2:11, RSVCE).

At the pool of Bethesda, Jesus healed a man who had been ill for thirty-eight years. After the physical healing, Jesus found the man later in the temple and said, "See, you are well! Sin no more, that nothing worse befall you" (John 5:14, RSVCE). Jesus' call to "sin no more" shows again that the true reason for healing is found in the sinner's moral transformation.

While the New Testament uses many words to describe the miraculous, St. John's word of choice is "sign." This is because the evangelist wants to ensure that every element of superstition is eliminated from the readers' minds. He wants to show that Christ's miracles are signs of something deeper going on. A pattern for the process can be seen when Jesus heals a man blind from birth (John 9:3).

Through his interaction with Jesus and the "sign" done on his behalf, the man moves from blindness to sight—a physical change—to insight—a spiritual change.

In the Acts of the Apostles, we see the apostles continuing this same ministry of miracles that call for spiritual change. Thus, Peter and John heal a crippled beggar at the temple gate, and afterward, Peter addresses the crowd, admonishing: "Repent therefore, and turn again, that your sins may be blotted out" (3:19, RSVCE).

Even a cursory reading of the New Testament makes it clear that miracles are not really focused on the physical dimension of life. They don't act so much as "proof" of Christ's divinity as they are "pointers" to follow Him. By prioritizing the necessity of faith, trust, repentance, and transformation, Jesus showed that the inner change of character was the true miracle He was after. Physical miracles served as an outward demonstration of the invisible and more essential healing He came to offer—a healing of the soul.

This also explains why actual, authenticated miracles are so rare. It explains why God doesn't make a blazing red cross appear in the night sky so the secular masses can see His glory. It explains why people born without limbs never see those limbs magically sprout before their eyes, as in some science-fiction movie. If people witnessed spectacles of that kind, they would be *forced* to believe. After all, who needs faith in the face of such obvious displays of power? Miracles such as these don't encourage faith—they destroy faith. They replace faith with knowledge.

But God doesn't want to replace faith with knowledge. He wants us to *trust* Him. He doesn't want to give us scientific, empirical proofs. His actions always work persuasively rather than coercively, allowing individuals to choose Him freely rather than be compelled through constant interventions in the natural order. The key to understanding this whole subject is that the purpose of miracles is not merely to provide physical healing but to serve a higher spiritual and faith-building objective.

Case in point. I have a friend who received a somewhat miraculous healing from God. It wasn't an overly forceful display of God's power. But it was miraculous nonetheless. At the time, she was in college, not living a particularly holy life, having a little too much fun, and flunking out. One winter day, she got into a terrible car accident that damaged several of her internal organs and shattered her pelvis and femur. In order to fix her leg, the doctors had to insert a long metal pin from her knee to her hip. The recovery was very difficult. To make matters worse, about a year after the accident, the pin in her leg inexplicably shifted and started to grind into her hip. The pain was excruciating, and she had to remain completely still in bed. An X-ray showed that surgery was required to remove the pin.

Just before the surgery, however, there was a knock on her door. It was a deacon and his wife from the local church. They explained that God had told them to go pray for her. Naturally, my friend felt uncomfortable about these strangers barging into her room and making this unusual request. But they persisted, and my friend allowed them to pray over her while she silently fumed.

But then, something amazing happened. After finishing the prayer, the deacon asked my friend to put her legs over the side of the bed and step onto the floor. When she did, she immediately felt a "click" in her hip. The pin had somehow righted itself and snapped into place. All the pain vanished, and she was literally able to dance around the room. The doctors couldn't believe what had happened.

For a long time, my friend wondered why God had done this for her. After all, so many people in the world were suffering from cancer and other life-threatening diseases. Why hadn't God helped them? What was His purpose in healing her leg injury, when it might have been fixed by surgery?

The answer goes to the heart of what we've been discussing. God always has something deeper in mind when He performs miracles. In this case, He wanted to show my friend that it was time for *her* to change. He wasn't interested so much in realigning the pin in her leg. He wanted to *realign her life*. By miraculously pointing the pin in the right direction, He wasn't overwhelming her with His power, but He was giving her a divine nudge to point herself in the right direction too.

And she did. My friend not only became serious about her Faith; she also went on to become a highly respected Catholic author and editor. In fact, she is the editor of this book on miracles that you're reading now![32]

Do you understand what I'm getting at? If you need a miracle—especially a healing of some kind—you need

[32] Heidi Hess Saxton, "A Miracle in My Life," *Substack*, September 8, 2024, https://substack.com/inbox/post/148501943. Heidi is a writer and editor whose blog, *Life on the Road Less Traveled*, reflects on faith, family, and personal growth. Visit her blog at https://heidisaxton.com/prayerstories/ and her Amazon author page at https://www.amazon.com/stores/Heidi-Hess-Saxton/author/B001K8HCOI.

to look inside yourself and see if there's something else that needs to be healed too. What is it about your own character that God might want you to change?

Indeed, the most profound "healing" in the Gospels was not a miracle but, rather, the dramatic change of character that takes place in the parable of the prodigal son. We all know the story about the young man who demanded his inheritance from his father and then spent it on riotous living. When he had wasted his money and was despondent and starving, he finally came to his senses, returned to his father, and said, "Father, I have sinned against Heaven and before you." And the father, instead of reprimanding him, welcomed him back with open arms, killed the fatted calf, threw him a huge celebration, put a ring on his finger and shoes on his feet, crying, " [My son] was dead, and is alive; he was lost, and is found" (Luke 15:11–32, RSVCE).

Herein lies the most efficacious method of increasing your chances of getting the miracle you desire: *you must die to yourself and be reborn a new person.*

The prodigal son repented and underwent a complete moral transformation. He changed his ways and went back home. As a reward, his father showered blessings upon him. You and I are worthy of miracles only if we are ready and willing to change our ways. That is the single most accurate barometer for measuring how we are responding to Jesus, and the single most important "condition" for obtaining miracles. Even "faith" in Jesus is important only insofar as it leads to greater union with God—and that union comes about only through repentance and transformation.

Bear in mind, I'm not talking here about the empty promises people so often and so passionately make to God whenever they're scared—only to break those promises the moment their fear abates. No, I'm talking about something much deeper. I'm talking about true repentance.

Let's discuss the subject of repentance more.

Often, we hear people say: "Be yourself." It's a phrase that sounds so inspirational and empowering. But the problem with this cliché is that we are *not* called to be ourselves. We are called to be our *best* selves. If you are a mature person and have accumulated the slightest bit of wisdom in life, you know that the way you are now is not necessarily your best self. You know you have flaws. You know the toxic thoughts and desires that are buzzing around your brain—possibly at this second. Isn't it true that you can imagine a better you? If so, it means there is room for you to transform yourself.

Or sometimes we hear Shakespeare's famous line from *Hamlet* used as self-improvement advice: "This above all, to thine own self be true."[33] Again, that sounds wonderfully philosophical. The difficulty is that if you are holding on to ideas that are false—even ideas that you've held for decades—that's not really being true to yourself. That's maintaining a false and distorted self. In fact, if you don't change the pattern of your behavior and try to grow in spiritual union with God, you might even be destroying yourself.

Your "true self" is found only in Jesus Christ. Indeed, that's the whole point of being a Christian. As you try to lead a virtuous, faith-filled life, Christ reveals to you who your true self is—and then you can strive even harder to become that person. When the prodigal son came to his senses, he realized he had to break away from his past self and return to his father. That's exactly what you and I are called to do. It's not enough to have a guilty conscience about the bad things we've done in the past. It's not enough that our conscience is bothering us. Plenty of people with guilty consciences continue their bad behavior. What's necessary is to break away from our past and renounce our sins.

[33] William Shakespeare, *Hamlet*, act 1, scene 3, line 84.

Sinning is something that's so misunderstood today. We need to talk more about it because it is the key to self-transformation. Sinning, simply defined, is the act of offending God. It's doing things that are wrong in *God's* eyes, not necessarily in *our* eyes. Sinning causes a kind of spiritual chaos in our soul—a disintegration, a division. It separates us on three levels. First, it separates us from ourselves—from who we truly are in God's eyes. Second, it separates us from other people, causing friction and sometimes even havoc in our personal relationships. Finally, it separates us from God, who is the very opposite of sin.[34]

Every single time we sin, these three divisions take place—and it affects us. Christ said that a house divided against itself cannot stand (Mark 3:25). So, what do you think happens when we keep chopping ourselves up in this fashion over a long period? We hurt ourselves badly. We collapse. We implode. No one has to tell us to feel unhappy. No one has to tell us to feel guilty. It happens on its own—because it's built into our very nature.

[34] For an extended treatment of this subject, see DeStefano, *30 Days to Your New Life*, chap. 16, "Getting Straight with God."

Now, what we do with those guilty feelings is our choice. This is where we face some crucial decisions because guilt can either harm us or help us grow. Some people try to ignore their guilt and learn to live with it. After all, we can get used to almost anything in life. But it's tough. The guilt is always lurking beneath the surface, gnawing at us, often without our even realizing why. It's like having termites in your house—they can eat away at the wooden structure for years without being noticed. You can spend a fortune remodeling the exterior, making everything look perfect from the outside. But underneath that shiny surface, the whole structure is falling apart.

That's exactly what some people do to themselves. They earn lots of money and achieve great success in the eyes of the world, yet they're still unhappy. They turn to psychologists or personal development courses and might make some progress for a while, but once the initial excitement fades, they're just as unhappy as before. The reason is that they haven't tackled the root problem—not just their guilt but the sins causing it.

Some people recognize that they've done something wrong and feel regret, but it's a regret that stays on the surface. They aren't sorry for the wrong itself—just for the consequences they now face or for getting caught. So they end up feeling foolish, frustrated, and angry at themselves.

When people experience this type of regret, their focus turns inward, fixating on their mistakes. Have you ever done that? Have you ever replayed your sins in your head over and over, like a broken record, until you're trapped in a cycle of hopeless remorse? There's no way out of that kind of thinking. It's an exhausting loop of frustration and self-condemnation. Many live their lives stuck in this rut, content to wallow in their guilt, lying helpless in the mud, without ever really trying to get up and break free.

Finally, there are people who take a sensible approach — a Christian approach. These people recognize their wrong-doing and regret it, but they don't get lost in their own guilt. Instead of being consumed by their mistakes, they look beyond themselves and turn to God. Rather than letting regret spiral into despair, they lift their eyes to Heaven and say, "Lord, I'm sorry. Please forgive me and help me find my way back to You." They make a conscious choice — rooted in faith and trust in God's mercy — to confess their sins and ask for His forgiveness. And guess what? God forgives them. Every single time.

You see, there's a delicate balance required here — a balance the world usually forgets. A mature person — whether he's religious or not—should have a reasonable amount of shame for the bad things he has done without an unreasonable burden of guilt. That's the tightrope that must be walked, and it can be walked successfully only if you know what to do with your sins once you've committed them.

The bottom line is, once you get over your pride, being forgiven for your sins is the easiest thing in the world. One drop of Christ's blood is enough to wash away the sins of a billion universes. Indeed, Christ completed the hardest part of the work Himself, on your behalf, a long time ago, by dying on the Cross. He opened the door so that your sins could be forgiven. He gave you the antidote to sin. Your role in the whole process is relatively simple. All you have to do, in essence, is walk through the door; all you have to do is swallow the antidote. And the way to do both those things is to be sorry and confess your sins to God and renounce them.

Now, if you're a Catholic, you have an added obligation of going to Confession—of making use of the sacrament of Reconciliation. Catholics believe that Christ Himself instituted this sacrament when He lived and walked in Palestine two thousand years ago. At that time, after He breathed on the apostles—a sign that He was giving them the Holy Spirit—He said to them: "If you forgive the sins of any, they are forgiven; if you retain the sins of any, they are retained" (John 20:23, RSVCE). Later, St. Paul confirmed this authority to forgive sins, when he said: "All this is from God, who through Christ reconciled us to himself and gave us the ministry of reconciliation" (2 Cor. 5:18, RSVCE).

No matter what religion you practice, though, there's really nothing more important that you can do than ask God for forgiveness. Does that mean you're going to be suddenly perfect? Of course not. God doesn't expect you to turn into a saint overnight. After you repent, you're going to experience setbacks and falls and lapses in the spiritual life. You're going to continue contending with pride and carnality and the other deadly sins. You're always going to have to deal with the possibility of habitual or compulsive problems and the things in life that trigger such behavior. But no matter what you do, as long as you sincerely desire to turn back to God, you can be forgiven. That's what God expects from you: to have in your heart the sincere intention of changing. Just like the prodigal son, you have to go back to your Father, express your willingness to amend your ways, be willing to do penance, and realize that you can't change on your own, that you don't have the power to change without the help of your Father.

Please understand that I'm not talking about mere self-improvement. Our objective isn't only to change this fault or that bad habit. And we're not talking about "negotiating with God," telling Him you're going to stop your sinful ways if you can get something from Him in return. For a Christian, repentance and transformation go much deeper than that. Christ wants you to really "die to your old self," in order for you to become your true best self. This is the meaning of the paradox: if you want to gain your life, you must first lose it. And it is also what it means that you must be "born again" (John 3:3).

So, to summarize, why did God create the world and everyone in it?

To share His love.

Why does God perform miracles, big and small?

To make us realize that God is the source of all good things, to increase our faith in Him so we will repent, transform, grow in union with Him, and help others do the same, so that we can all share His love here and, later, in the world to come.

Are you on board with that plan? Are you ready to change? Really ready? If so, you've improved your chances of gaining a miracle a hundredfold because you've plugged yourself into the very source and purpose of miracles.

With that in mind, here's another petition to add to your miracle prayer:

Lord, help me to repent of all my past sins and die to myself, for the purpose of transforming into my best, true self—the person You created me to be and someone worthy of receiving Your miraculous assistance.

9

Personal Relationship versus Community

In the last chapter, we talked about the need to transform into your best self. But we aren't quite done with that subject. The essence of Christian transformation is something that Protestants and Catholics agree on—the need to have a personal relationship with Jesus Christ. This idea of "relationship" is crucial because it has the power to turn a mere set of beliefs into a living, dynamic, intimate connection with God. Both Catholic and Protestant perspectives converge on the point that it is through this relationship that believers find the meaning, purpose, and strength to live out their faith daily.

Protestants often highlight the subjective dimension of this connection, focusing on private, personal prayer, Bible reading, and the sense of walking with Jesus as a friend and guide in everyday life. This approach emphasizes the immediacy and accessibility of Jesus, encouraging believers to converse with Him directly and to seek His guidance in all aspects of life. St. Paul often talks about knowing Christ personally in this way (e.g., Phil. 2:6–11; Col. 1:12–20).

For Catholics, this relationship has the same subjective element, but it is also profoundly nurtured through the sacraments, especially Reconciliation (which we just spoke about) and the Eucharist.

Through the sacrament of the Eucharist, Catholics receive Jesus in a tangible way, which they consider the most intimate personal encounter possible (John 6:48–63). Thus, the sacramental life is not just about ritual but about entering into a deeper communion with Jesus. The Eucharist is considered the "source and summit of the Christian life" because it contains "the whole spiritual good of the Church"—indeed, it contains Christ Himself (CCC 1324).

The Catholic Church teaches that the Eucharist is really and truly God. It is *God made man.* It is the *Body, Blood, Soul, and Divinity* of Jesus Christ. It is not a symbol and not just a recollection of past events. It is the Lord, miraculously present—and also miraculously hidden—under the appearances of bread and wine. That's why the miracle that happens at the moment of consecration during the Catholic Mass is called *transubstantiation*—the transfer of the substance of bread and wine into the *substance* of the Body and Blood of Christ. If you've ever received Communion at a Catholic Mass, understand that, in doing so, you have not eaten bread or drunk wine. You have taken God into your own body.

Jesus said: "He who eats my flesh and drinks my blood abides in me, and I in him" (John 6:56, RSVCE). Catholics believe this *literally*. They believe that Christ meant that He gives Himself to us in the Eucharist as spiritual nourishment. By consuming His Body and Blood, we become united to the person of Christ, and in being united to Christ, we are united not only to His humanity but also to His *divinity*. Our mortal and corruptible nature is transformed by being joined to the source of all life—indeed, to Life itself.

In everyday language, this translates into: *You are what you eat.*[35]

Think about it. When you consume things that are bad for you, such as sugar, candy, fast food, and junk food, your body is negatively affected. Not only will you get heavy, but you'll start having all kinds of health problems. It's

---

[35] For a similar treatment of this subject, see DeStefano, *30 Days to Your New Life*, chap. 24, "The Time Machine."

a simple fact that the worse you eat, the more your body deteriorates. But the opposite is also true. If you drink lots of water and eat lots of vegetables and nutritious whole foods, chock-full of essential vitamins and minerals and antioxidants, your physiology improves — not only on the outside but on a cellular and molecular level.

Well, what do you think happens if you consume God? Catholics believe that if you receive Communion on a regular basis, in a morally upright, worthy, faith-filled manner, you're going to become more like God. You're going to be lifted into a higher kind of life, a life that Christ described in the Gospels as "the Kingdom of Heaven" (Matt. 13). This is not only a life of increased virtue but a life of great power — power to follow the Golden Rule, power to love your enemies, power to bring peace wherever there is strife, power to accomplish things that seem impossible; a life characterized by humility, truth, beauty, goodness, extraordinary closeness to God, and, yes, miracles.

Because of its incredible power, Catholic churches often expose the Eucharist for worship on a regular basis. Some even have separate chapels set aside for Eucharistic adoration. Many of these chapels are open twenty-four hours a day. That means that if you have a problem — one that is keeping you up late into the night—you can get in your car and go directly to see Jesus and kneel before Him: the same Lord who walked in Palestine two thousand years ago, really present in the Blessed Sacrament. Talk about consoling friendship and intimacy! I can assure you that if you speak to Jesus in person like this on a regular basis, miracles are going to start happening in your life, whether you ask for them or not.

Here's another Fr. Brian story: A few years ago, an old woman in Fr. Brian's parish was in the final stages of cancer. The doctors let her go home to receive hospice care. She wasn't expected to live through the week. The woman's husband asked Fr. Brian to come over to the house to give his wife the sacrament of the Anointing of the Sick—which used to be called "Last Rites." This sacrament is a powerful rite intended for those who are seriously ill, elderly, or near death. It brings spiritual healing and sometimes physical healing as well.

Fr. Brian went immediately and entered the lady's room, where she lay, barely conscious, on what was surely her deathbed. He administered the sacrament and was able to put a tiny particle of the Eucharist on the woman's tongue. After he finished, the priest left the room with the husband, who offered to give him something to eat.

Suddenly, they heard a voice coming from the woman's bedroom. They rushed in and were shocked to see that the woman had opened her eyes. She looked at them and said, in a hoarse voice, "I smell turkey. Can I have a turkey sandwich?" Astonished, the woman's husband immediately turned to go to the kitchen to make the sandwich, but the woman stopped him, saying, "No, I feel like getting out of bed." So, the two men helped her put on a robe and walked her into the kitchen, where she sat down at the table and proceeded to eat not only a turkey sandwich but some cookies too. It turned out the woman's cancer had gone into spontaneous remission.

The irony is that, two weeks later, Fr. Brian caught double pneumonia and had to be taken to the hospital. While he was recovering, the old woman visited him, bringing a tin of cookies she had made!

Never underestimate the power of the sacraments of the Church—especially the Eucharist—when it comes to fostering an intimate, personal, powerful, and *healing* relationship with Jesus Christ.

On the other hand, as central as this belief is, Jesus was clear that the Kingdom of Heaven is more than just a personal relationship. There's something else that's critical, and that something also plays a role in obtaining miracles.

It's called the community of believers. To be a Christian means that you're part of a wider family.

Think about it. When Jesus taught us to pray, He didn't tell us to say, "My Father, who art in Heaven"; He told us to say, "*Our* Father" (Matt 6:9). He also said to His disciples, "Where *two or three* gather in my name, there am I with them" (Matt. 18:20). This is what St. Paul was referring to when he spoke so often of the *Body of Christ*.[36] It's a concept that emphasizes the interdependence of all Christians, in which every member contributes to the health and growth of the Church as a whole, with Christ at the head as the source of life and direction.

Thus, believing in God is not strictly a one-on-one affair. It involves the whole community of believers. Having a personal relationship with the Lord—while essential—is never an excuse for self-absorption, self-centeredness, and isolation. It's no accident that the symbol of our Faith isn't a circle or some other closed figure but, rather, a cross, with its beams extending outward in all directions—to all four corners of the globe and even beyond that, into the

[36] 1 Cor. 12:12–27; Eph. 4:4–16; Col. 1:18; Eph. 1:22-23; Rom. 12:4–5.

next world. To be a Christian, by definition, means to go *out* of yourself and not just to retreat inward.

This leads to yet another paradoxical proposition. While it's paramount to foster a personal relationship with the Lord, often in silence and solitude and with intimate communication and contact, we know that a communal relationship with our neighbors, directed toward God, is just as important. This interconnectedness within the Church plays a significant role in the Christian life. These aspects of spirituality operate in seemingly opposite manners, but they are both necessary.

This applies especially to prayer. So-called intercessory prayer is a central aspect of the Christian religion. When we pray for others, we are exercising love, aligning ourselves with God's will, and actively building up the Body of Christ. Intercessory prayer reflects our unity as Christians and our shared mission to support each other in faith.

Protestants and Catholics alike believe in the power of intercessory prayer. It's common in Protestant churches to ask friends, family members, and worship leaders to pray for each other's needs — for strength, guidance, peace, safety, abundance, encouragement, and unity.

Catholics do this, too, but we extend the practice by including the saints. Remember, the saints are people who have died and gone to Heaven. Catholics have always believed that the prayers of the saints can be particularly powerful. Protestants often object to this practice on two grounds: first, that we should not "pray to the dead," since they believe this is condemned by the Bible; and second, that Jesus is the one Mediator between God and humanity, and there can be no others.

Catholics have answers to both these objections. In the first case, it's true that biblical texts such as Deuteronomy 18:10-11 and Isaiah 19:3 say that "communication with the dead" is forbidden. But what is forbidden in these verses is "conjuring up" the dead through mediums. The Church has always condemned that practice very forcefully. But "conjuring up" the dead is completely different from asking for the intercession of brothers and sisters in Christ who are in Heaven. Indeed, we know that the saints are *not* dead but are alive in Christ Jesus. The Catholic perspective, supported by Scripture and Tradition, holds that the saints are with God in Heaven and are actively participating in His divine plan. Revelation 5:8 and 8:3-4 depict the saints offering our prayers to God, indicating their role in the heavenly ministry of intercessory prayer before God's throne.

Regarding the fact that Jesus Christ is the one Mediator between God and humanity (1 Tim. 2:5), Catholics again agree. We hold, however, that this does not exclude others from *participating* in Jesus' role as Mediator through intercessory prayer. After all, Protestants wholeheartedly endorse the idea that we can ask our family and friends to pray for us, thereby giving them the ability to participate in Christ's mediation. Catholics simply broaden this circle to include the saints, who are even more alive than our friends and family on earth and are even closer to the Lord. That makes their prayers especially powerful (James 5:16).

The bottom line is this: If you can ask your sister to pray for you, why can't you ask a saint in Heaven to pray for you? After all, the saints are not sitting around in Heaven doing nothing. They are aware, conscious, and active. In fact, they are more active than we are because they are not limited and encumbered by their physical bodies. To some extent, they are able to see and know things about our lives on earth—including our troubles. The fact that they are spirits (and will continue to be until the resurrection) doesn't matter. They still have powers—one of which is the power to pray for us.

Which brings us back to the subject of miracles.

Intercessory prayer is an incredibly important factor in many miraculous occurrences, as vividly illustrated in the Gospels. There's the story of Lazarus, for example, who was raised from the dead after his sisters, Mary and Martha, called upon Jesus for help (John 11:1-44). There's the story of Jairus, a synagogue leader who begged Jesus to heal his dying daughter; and when she died, Jesus brought her back to life (Mark 5:21-24, 35-43). We also see this dynamic at work in the healing of the centurion's servant, the Syrophoenician woman's daughter, and the nobleman's son, among others (Matt. 8:5-13; Mark 7:24-30; John 4:46-54). These events show that Jesus' miracles often came about not because of the faith of those in need but because of the faith of *others* who interceded for them.

Thus, when we pray for our friends and family—or when they pray for us—we are participating in a biblically based, theologically sound way of bringing about the miraculous.

What does all this mean? If you need a miracle, you shouldn't keep it a secret! You should ask everyone you know to pray for it. You should shout your request from the rooftops—or from whatever social media platforms you have. Your objective is to get as many people praying for your intention as possible. That doesn't mean you have to divulge every detail of your personal life to those around you, but you shouldn't hesitate to ask them to pray for a "special intention" you have. When they do, God will know they are praying for your miracle.

And while you're asking your friends and relatives for help, you should go to the saints as well.

Catholics have patron saints who serve as special protectors and guardians over various aspects of life, from health issues to financial concerns to family matters. This practice is deeply rooted in the understanding that the saints, who have led exemplary lives of faith and are now in Heaven, can intercede for us in specific ways that align with both their earthly experiences and their heavenly missions.

Each saint has a unique story and patronage that makes him or her especially suited to interceding in a particular way and a particular area. For instance, St. Blaise is invoked for throat ailments because he miraculously saved a boy from choking. St. Matthew is invoked for financial troubles because in life he was a tax collector. St. Peregrine is invoked by cancer patients because he was miraculously cured of his cancer while praying before a crucifix the night before he was due to have his leg amputated. At the end of this book, I've included an appendix listing the patron saints for all the major miracles for which people usually pray. Be sure to read through it carefully and enlist the help of the saint or saints in Heaven who can best assist you with your specific request.

Remember, praying to patron saints is not about bypassing Jesus but, rather, about seeking support and intercession from our *extended spiritual family*. The saints, as righteous individuals who have finished their earthly race, can offer their perfected prayers alongside ours, amplifying our petitions before God. Asking them for help is a way of showing God that you understand and embrace the paradox of personal relationship versus community relationship in the Body of Christ.

And finally, we must never forget the Blessed Virgin Mary. Our Lady is the patron saint of *all humanity*. Catholics believe that every human being has two mothers: an earthly mother and a spiritual mother. We believe that Christ gave Mary to us as our spiritual mother when He was hanging on the Cross on Calvary (John 19:27).

To my brother and sister Christians, I want to repeat most sincerely: Catholics do *not* worship Mary. We understand that she is a created human being. We understand that, compared with Our Lord, she is *infinitesimal* in value. But we do revere her. We do venerate her. We do honor her.

Moreover, we know that Mary is, by far, our most important intercessor when we need a miracle, and this belief is deeply rooted in Catholic theology and Scripture. Mary, as the Mother of God, holds a unique and privileged position in Heaven. She is not just another saint; she is the Queen of saints, the Queen of angels, the Queen of Heaven itself. She is the "spouse" of the Holy Spirit (Luke 1:35). She is the very means by which the Incarnation took place, and she is the Woman of Revelation 12:1, clothed with the sun and the sign of the Church in glory. She is the person closest to her Son, Jesus Christ.

It is not an exaggeration to say that Mary's whole life was a miracle. Consider the following:

- ❖ According to the Catholic Church, Mary was uniquely free from Original Sin from the moment she was conceived, a belief known as the miracle of the Immaculate Conception.
- ❖ Catholics are not unique in reverencing Mary. Muslims, too, hold that Mary was perfect from her conception onward and that God miraculously granted her special grace to live a flawless life.
- ❖ All Christians and Muslims share the belief in the miracle of the Virgin Birth: Mary conceived Jesus Christ in her womb as a virgin by the power of the Holy Spirit. The Bible tells us that the

archangel Gabriel visited Mary to reveal God's plan for her to be Jesus' Mother. Luke 1:34–35 recounts part of their conversation:

> "How can this be," Mary asked the angel, "since I am a virgin?" The angel answered, "The Holy Spirit will come on you, and the power of the Most High will overshadow you. So the holy one to be born will be called the Son of God."

❖ Since all Christians believe that Jesus Christ is God made man, they see Mary's pregnancy and Jesus' birth as part of the miraculous event known as the Incarnation, when God came into the suffering world to save it.

❖ Finally, Catholic and Orthodox Christians hold that Mary entered Heaven in a miraculous way when her life on earth was completed. Catholics believe in the miracle of the Assumption: that Mary was taken body and soul into Heaven—they do not specify whether she died. Orthodox Christians believe in the miracle of Dormition: that Mary died naturally, but that her soul went to Heaven and her body stayed on earth for three days before being resurrected and taken up into Heaven.

For miracle seekers, probably the most important Bible story about Mary's life on earth is that of the wedding feast at Cana. It was at Mary's request that Jesus performed His first public miracle—turning water into wine—even though He initially told her that His time had "not yet come" (John 2:1-11). In other words, Our Lord performed a great miracle because of a request from His mother—a miracle that started Him on the road to the Cross and one that He initially seemed unwilling to perform. Despite His reluctance, Jesus obeyed Mary, highlighting the special relationship they shared and continue to share in Heaven.

Mary is not just the Mother of God and the Mother of the Church; she is the *Mother of miracles*. Indeed, in the history of the Church, there have been countless reported miracles due to Mary's intercession. These include the well-known Marian apparitions—such as at Lourdes, Fátima, Guadalupe, Knock, and Akita—times when believers say Mary miraculously appeared on earth to deliver messages, encourage love for God, call sinners to repentance, and bestow the gift of healing. Moreover, many Catholics think that Mary has a key role to play in dispensing God's graces. Though this is not a defined dogma, some of the greatest saints and popes in history have taught it as an article of faith. What does it mean?

We know that the saints in Heaven are very active and that each one of them has a unique role to play in God's divine plan. Mary, by virtue of her special place in salvation history and her unique role as the spouse of the Holy Spirit, has a special job in Heaven too: the distribution of God's graces. In other words, all the graces God has wanted to give us from all eternity as part of His providence—including all His miracles and answered prayers—must pass through Our Lady's hands to come to us. If that belief is true—and I wholeheartedly think it is—Mary is not only the most vital intercessor we can turn to in times of trouble, but she is also the very conduit of *all* divine assistance.

When my friend Fr. Brian was a seminarian at Mount St. Mary's in Emmitsburg, Maryland, he had very little money. In fact, he had accumulated quite a bit of credit card debt in paying his basic living expenses. When his money ran out and all his bills were due, as well as his tuition, he was forced to make a very painful decision: to take a leave of absence from the seminary. He was distraught.

On the day he was planning to tell the rector he was leaving, he went up to the National Shrine Grotto of Our Lady of Lourdes, on the grounds of Mount St. Mary's. The grotto is the oldest replica of the site where Our Lady appeared to St. Bernadette in Lourdes, France. Kneeling before the statue of Our Lady, Fr. Brian said a very simple prayer: "Mary, if your Son wants me to be a priest, can you please ask Him to help me?" Then he went back to the seminary. To his surprise, the rector was waiting for him outside his room. He had an envelope that he immediately thrust into Fr. Brian's hands, saying, "This is for you." It was full of cash. Apparently, a benefactor of the seminary had sent a large donation to the rector and asked him to use it however he needed, including for distribution to needy seminarians. For some reason, the rector immediately thought of Fr. Brian. This was remarkable because, though the rector had information on the finances of all his seminarians, he had no idea how dire Fr. Brian's situation was. He certainly didn't know he was about to take a leave of absence. When Fr. Brian opened the envelope, he counted the money and realized that it was exactly what was needed to pay his bills and to get him through the next semester. The envelope also contained a prayer card from the donor that said: "Come to the grotto and pray."

It has been close to forty years since that day, and, in that time, Fr. Brian has been very busy doing the Lord's work—including accomplishing the miraculous.

So, if you need a miracle right now, and you've tried everything, it's time to put the Blessed Virgin Mary at the top of your list. If the Lord seems reluctant to say yes to you, ask His Mother to intercede with Him, as she did at Cana and so many other times in history. That may be exactly what He's waiting for to grant your request.

To do this, you can add the following petition to the miracle prayer you've been saying:

Lord, strengthen my personal relationship with You — especially through the worthy reception of the Blessed Sacrament — as well as the relationship I have with You through the Body of Christ. I ask my brother and sister Christians on earth and in Heaven, especially the Blessed Virgin Mary, to intercede on my behalf for the miracle I am requesting.

10

Precision in Prayer versus Openness to God's Will

When we feel desperate because of some profound problem we're experiencing, it's natural to approach God with a very precise request to address that problem. Indeed, it's good to be precise when we ask God for miracles. God *wants* us to be precise.

The Bible offers many examples of the value of precision in our prayers and of how much God cares about the most minute aspects of our lives. As Jesus said, "Even the hairs of your head are all numbered" (Luke 12:7, RSVCE).

Why does God appreciate precise prayers? From a theological perspective, there are several reasons. First, precision in prayer shows that we trust God with the intricate details of our lives, as we would with a close friend or family member. If our goal as Christians is to grow in our relationship with Christ, it makes sense to talk to Him about these details. It makes sense for us to go to Him with everything that's on our minds. That's what real relationships are all about—sharing.

Moreover, when we make specific requests, we acknowledge God's ultimate sovereignty over *all* facets of our lives. We acknowledge that He is not just Lord of the church we belong to. He is Lord of our families, Lord of our workplaces, Lord of our neighborhoods, Lord of our vacations, Lord of our bank accounts, Lord of our bodies, Lord of our bedrooms. Miracle requests that pertain to these areas demonstrate our faith in God's willingness to provide for even our smallest needs, and our understanding that God views our lives not with a long telescope from Heaven but, rather, from a front-row seat.

Being precise also helps *us* to focus with clarity on our needs and desires. Though we're often mistaken in what we truly want (as we discussed in chapter 4), if we reflect more conscientiously on what we are asking and pray with more spiritual discernment, it could have the effect of aligning our hearts more closely with God's will.

Finally, when specific prayers are answered, it becomes a powerful testimony to God's action in our lives and showcases His responsiveness to the things we care most about. It shows how God loves us so much that He is not too proud to reach down from Heaven into the minutiae of our lives and "get His hands dirty," so to speak. Thus, answers to precise prayers encourage our faith and the faith of those around us.

But here we come to the last of God's miracle paradoxes, and in many ways, the most important of all. For while it's praiseworthy and beneficial to be precise in our prayers, we must also understand that the essence of prayer isn't about enforcing our will but about opening ourselves up to the will of God, which often unfolds in ways we least expect. Therefore, we are called to be precise and yet, simultaneously, completely open to how God chooses to address our precision.

This concept of openness is crucial. In fact, it's the key to understanding why miraculous answers to prayers occur all the time, even when we don't realize it.

Earlier in this book, I related a few personal experiences I've had with "unanswered" miracle prayers. But I never explained how those situations turned out. Let me do that now.

I mentioned that when I was a boy, I wanted to become a doctor—specifically, a heart surgeon. I prayed intensely for this goal, even though I wasn't religious. But when that didn't work out, I devoted myself to another dream: political success. I decided that I would work in various campaigns, in the hope that they would put me on a path to running for elective office. I had aspirations of one day making a big impact on the lives of all the people I represented. Again, even though I wasn't religious, I prayed hard to achieve this objective. Yet I failed again.

God had "refused" me twice, but by then I was older and really lost in the wilderness. I didn't know what I was going to do with my life. So I went back to yet another ambition: to become a writer. But I didn't know what kind of writer I wanted to be. I tried everything—speeches, history textbooks, journalism. No matter what I attempted, I had minimal success and wasn't truly inspired. Then, sometime in my twenties, after years of being away from the Faith, I started to get more interested in Christianity. About that time, I read a book by C. S. Lewis called *The Screwtape Letters*, and it made a powerful impression on me. It was the first time I had ever read anything spiritual that made me laugh and think at the same time.

I suddenly realized that maybe there was a way I could combine *all* the ambitions of my life. Maybe God had given me the desire to be a doctor and a public servant and a writer for the same reason. If I could write books like *The Screwtape Letters* (not as good, of course), perhaps I could still have what I always wanted. Perhaps I could assist people who needed help—not through surgery or political legislation—but through writing.

That was an epiphany for me. For so many years, I wanted to be a doctor. Then, for years after that, I wanted a political career. But I was wrong. My true desire was to be a *healer*. But like many other people who pray for a miracle, I didn't realize what my true desire was. So, when I asked God to grant me specific things, I naturally asked for the *wrong* things. God saw through my superficial words and feelings and, using His divine vision, penetrated deep into my soul and saw what I was really after.

Twenty years and thirty books later, I'm still writing—and I couldn't imagine feeling more fulfilled.

Do you see my point? I'm happy that I prayed to God to help me achieve precise goals, but I wish I would have been mature enough and wise enough to be open to what God wanted to give me. Had I quietly and prayerfully *listened* more, had I had a spirit of openness to God's will, I wouldn't have gotten so upset, frustrated, and depressed when the specific prayers I requested were "denied." Instead, I would have said to myself, "Don't worry. God didn't say no to you. He said, 'Wait and see what I've got planned. It's so much better than what you *think* you want. In fact, I'm going to give you what you truly desire. Just give me more time to arrange things.'"

I also related a personal story about my father. I said that when he was in his early seventies, he was diagnosed with a terminal blood disease and given a little over a year to live. I was extremely distressed by this news and prayed fervently that he would outlive the doctors' predictions by at least a couple of years. Despite my prayers, pain, and pleading, my father passed away in fifteen months—exactly what the doctors had predicted.

It was obvious to me that God had denied the miracle I requested. Soon after my father passed, however, I realized something interesting. During his illness, I visited his house every day to talk to him. I also took him to his weekly hospital appointments for blood transfusions. As a result, my whole family spent a great deal of time together.

Now, in the years before my father's diagnosis, I would see him perhaps once every two weeks. Sometimes less than that. But over the fifteen months of his illness, I spent time with him every single day—much more than I would have spent with him otherwise. It's strange. At other points in my life, I could have never visited my father every day, because I was busy or traveling so much for work. But it just so happens that, this particular year, I was working close to home and my hours were flexible. Even though I was far from being a perfect son, I felt inspired to see my father every day. And during that period, our relationship deepened. We even had a few "breakthroughs" in terms of resolving old problems and animosities. We also shared many memorable moments, talking, joking, eating, smoking an occasional cigar, reminiscing about my childhood as well as his.

When I calculated the time I spent visiting my father before he got ill—once every two weeks—I realized that, in three years (the amount of time I had prayed he would live for), I would have seen him roughly 78 times. In contrast, visiting him every day for fifteen months—as I actually did—resulted in almost 450 visits. I had begged God for a miracle—that my father would live for three years instead of one—and even though he died in fifteen months, my 450 visits, if spaced out over two-week periods, would have added up to more than seventeen years!

What I'm trying to say is that I asked God for three years more with my father, and He gave me the equivalent of seventeen. So, He *did* answer my prayer. He *did* give me my miracle. Indeed, He gave me much more. First, He arranged all the myriad elements of my busy life so that I had the *time* to see my father. Then He gave me the *desire* to visit my father every day and the *patience* to deal diplomatically with many difficult problems that continually arose, owing to our strong personalities. In other words, God gave me a miracle, but He did so in a manner that went far beyond my initial request, providing me with a much more profound and meaningful answer. I realized it only afterward.

I also told the story of a little girl who died despite the fervent prayers of her family's church. When she passed, the members of the congregation went through a crisis of faith. It seemed to them that their request for a miracle was refused. And yes, it's true that the little girl died. But anytime we pray for someone to survive a terminal illness miraculously, the core reason we're praying is that we love the person and want what's best for him or her—and we assume that means living as long as possible. Indeed, if we're honest with ourselves, what we truly want is for that person to live *forever*.

Well, God hears that prayer, and sometimes the best way for Him to answer it is to bring that person home to Heaven *now*. Sometimes that's the best way to guarantee that he or she lives happily forever, despite the terrible grief caused to the family.

Yes, I know people don't want to hear this. Whenever a young person dies, it's very difficult to find any kind of blessing that results from the loss. But even in the midst of that kind of tragedy, when everyone is uttering empty words and clichés and sentiments that don't help in the slightest, the truth is still the truth. And the truth is that life is incredibly short for all of us. It goes by in a flash. No matter what age you live to, it's just a drop of water in the ocean of eternity. When a young girl dies, it's unspeakably painful, but the fact is that she is at least finished with the hardest part of life—the dying part. She has gotten something over with that all of us must still go through. And while enjoying good experiences can be a wonderful thing, having them ten times over by living longer doesn't make them any more fulfilling. The only thing that truly counts in life is getting to Heaven. If you die at six years old from cancer and become a saint, you've lived a magnificent life.

Try, for just a moment, to look at this tragedy from a divine perspective, and not a human one. If God, in His infinite wisdom, seeing the future clearly, determined that the best time to take the little girl into His arms was that particular moment, and not later, then no amount of praying could have ever changed His mind. We don't know what physical suffering or emotional heartache or spiritual dangers awaited that girl had she lived. Neither do we know what things might *not* have happened in the lives of other people if she remained alive. My mother had a miscarriage before she got pregnant with me. Had her unborn baby lived, I would never have come into the world, and you wouldn't be reading these words now. The same is true for my wife. Her mother had a miscarriage a few months before she was conceived. She would never have been born if her mom had given birth to the first child. We both owe our existence to two children who died—two children we will one day meet, hopefully, in Heaven. That doesn't mean our parents were wrong for being devastated by the loss of their unborn children. It just means that there was a bigger plan they couldn't see.

When that little girl died, the members of her congregation had trouble accepting that there was a bigger plan. They couldn't see with the eyes of faith that that was the *perfect time* for that child to enter Heaven. But God, in His wisdom, with His knowledge of the future, and through His permissive will, allowed the members of that congregation to learn a great lesson. To be authentic Christians, they *had* to learn the difference between emotionalism and faith, between praying with confidence, persistence, and precision, and really praying in Jesus' name—which means being radically open to the will of the Father. And while it's true that the faith of the congregation was shaken at first, it soon became strong again—stronger, in fact, than ever before. The deep relationships that were formed because of that searing experience, as well as the spiritual wisdom that was gained, and the love that was poured out in interceding for that little girl molded the congregation into a much stronger, more faithful, and more closely knit community of believers. Indeed, it wouldn't be an exaggeration to say that the little girl's death was responsible for the *birth* of a new, more genuinely Christlike fellowship—in the words of Henri Nouwen, a "fellowship of the broken."[37]

All of us have experienced tragedies in life. All of us have had prayers that were seemingly "refused" but were answered by God in ways we weren't expecting and that nevertheless conferred certain blessings upon us and those around us.

In fact, we don't need to recount any anecdotal evidence to demonstrate this point. All we have to do is

[37] Henri J. M. Nouwen, *Out of Solitude: Three Meditations on the Christian Life* (Notre Dame, IN: Ave Maria Press, 2004), 40–41.

go back to the New Testament. In it, we find the most significant and well known of all "prayer refusal" stories. I briefly mentioned it earlier. It's the one that occurred in the Garden of Gethsemane to Jesus Christ Himself (Matt. 26:36–46).

Remember, Christ is God the Son—the second Person of the Blessed Trinity. The night before He died, in His afflicted humanity, He prayed to His Father that He wouldn't have to endure the bloody, brutal death of a crucifixion. He knew very well how much pain He was going to endure, and He asked His Father, "If it is possible, let this cup be taken away from me" (Matt. 26:39).

In other words, though never wavering for a moment in His intention to redeem humanity—that part of Jesus' will in touch with the senses did ask for a last-minute reprieve from intense suffering. As the *Catechism of the Catholic Church* says, when that final moment of agony came, Christ expressed "the horror that death represented for His human nature" (CCC 612).

According to St. Thomas Aquinas, the will attached to the sensual aspect of Christ's soul recoiled from fear.[38] And it recoiled in an impassioned way. The Bible says

---

[38] Thomas Aquinas, *ST*, III, q. 18, art. 5, reply to obj. 1.

that Jesus felt His emotional agony so intensely that He sweat droplets of blood (Luke 22:44). But since He was the perfect Son, He added to His prayer, "Yet not as I will, but as You will" (Matt. 26:39).

We all know what happened. His request was denied. The Crucifixion went on as scheduled. What could be the meaning of the profound mystery of this refusal?

Now we must be careful here. Though this is a book of popular theology and not a strictly scholarly work, we don't want to risk being too loose in our language. We don't want to imply that there is any "duality" in the Person of Christ or that, before the Crucifixion, there was some kind of defection in Christ's human will from that of the divine will. In other words, we don't want to drift off into the age-old heresy of Nestorianism. No, the Father, the Son, and the Holy Spirit are three distinct Persons, but they are still one God.

Yet God the Incarnate Son *did* react in terror. He *did* ask His Father if there was a way to escape the pain He soon would be experiencing, and in this sense, the Father *did* say no to the pleas that arose from His very human soul.

We need to discuss this question before we end this book because it's really the focal point of everything we've talked about up to now.

In the way I have described it, Jesus Christ asked His Father if He could redeem humanity without having to experience intense suffering. But He made sure to prioritize the will of His Father—which necessitated that He die on the Cross. It was this unshakable determination to do the will of the Father—despite trembling in the face of fear—that resulted in the ultimate miracle of salvation. The question is: Was there no other, less painful, less bloody way to accomplish our redemption? Was there really a need for the Cross?

The answer, simply put, is yes. Not only was there a need for the Cross, but the Cross was the best and most perfect way to save humanity. It was also the best and most perfect way to answer Jesus' prayer.

Of course, God could have saved us by magically waving His hand and forgiving us for mankind's Original Sin in the Garden of Eden—and for all the other sins human beings have committed down through history until today. But that would have been an act of pure mercy, without any justice whatsoever. The Cross made it possible for us—human beings—to participate in our own redemption. It made it possible for a perfectly obedient man—Jesus Christ, the God-Man—to make up for the sin of disobedience of the first man—Adam. In other words, it made it possible for humanity to be redeemed in a perfectly just *and* perfectly merciful way, at the same time.

And it made it possible for other things as well. For instance, God knew that the Cross would become the central symbol of Christianity, and He knew it would contain all the truth we could ever hope to know about this beautiful, joyful, sorrowful, painful world in which we live.[39]

The Cross contains the truth that there *is* a God and that He is not merely some abstraction but a personal, caring Creator and Father. It contains the truth that He is a Father who loves us so much that He became one of us and even suffered death for us to make up for the sin of our first parents. It contains the truth that the key to life is love; the key to love is self-sacrifice; and the key to self-sacrifice is the surrender of our own will to the will of the Father.

The Cross contains the truth about how terrible sin really is. Christianity has always taught that one of the main reasons God became a man and endured such pain and anguish is that the consequences of sin require it. Christ's violent death shows in no uncertain terms that "the wages

[39] For a similar treatment of this subject, see Anthony DeStefano, *Inside the Atheist Mind* (Nashville: Thomas Nelson, 2018), chap. 10, "The End of the Atheists."

of sin is death" (Rom. 6:23). Whenever we rebel against God, whenever we go through some kind of terrible fear or guilt or grief or trial, we can always look at the Cross and say, "God hates sin and death so much that He went through *that* in order to save us. He went through *that* so we could be forgiven over and over again for committing the same sins. He went through *that* in order to give us everlasting life — just as long as we have faith in Him and turn back to Him when we fall."

The Cross also contains the truth about the mystery of evil in the world. After all, the greatest evil ever committed was the evil of the Crucifixion. That was, without question, the single most appalling act of ingratitude, deception, betrayal, depravity, obscenity, and malevolence of all time. God — the Creator of everything and everyone — was killed by His own creatures. The crime was not simply homicide or patricide or fratricide or even genocide. It was *deicide*. No evil in the universe could ever come close to the Crucifixion and death of Christ.

Yet what did God manage to do with the most monstrous of all human deeds?

Out of the darkness of the Crucifixion, He brought forth the light of the Resurrection. In a stunning and miraculous act of reversal, God turned evil on its head, redeeming mankind, elevating the human person to a divine level, making it possible for sins to be forgiven and for us to receive countless blessings during our earthly lifetime. On top of this, He threw open the gates of Heaven so that one day we could all be reunited with our friends and loved ones in an eternity of happiness.

Think about that for a minute. When Christ rose from the dead, it wasn't just His spirit that came back to life. His body was brought back to life too. It was His whole person. When He appeared to His apostles that first Easter morning, the same lungs that had been gasping for air on the Cross were breathing again. The same muscles that had been wracked with pain were moving again. The same heart that had stopped on Good Friday was beating again.

And it's still beating today, in Heaven.

That's what's going to happen to *you* too. Because of the death and Resurrection of Christ, you will one day rise from the dead. Because of the death and Resurrection of Christ, you will one day have a glorified body in Heaven. Because of the death and Resurrection of Christ, you can know that when you meet your departed friends and relatives there, you're going to be able to see them *in the flesh*. That means that if you're sad right now because your mother died, take heart. When you see her again in Heaven after the general resurrection, you won't be seeing a ghost. It will truly be your mother. You'll be able to run up to her and hug her and kiss her and feel the warmth of her skin and hear her voice again. That's what the Resurrection means. That's what awaits us in Heaven.

In Christ's dying for us on the Cross and rising from the dead, God didn't bring just a little good out of evil. He brought the greatest good out of the greatest evil. Because of this, we can know with certitude that God is able to bring good out of all the evils *we* experience in life—whether those evils are monstrous, such as the death of someone we love, or less painful, such as the fear of going bankrupt. It means that God can take every sad, cruel, unfair, and tragic thing that happens to us and somehow transform it into a blessing.

This is the truth about the mystery of suffering. This is the truth about the necessity of the Cross. This is the truth about the Resurrection. And this is the miracle that Jesus was granted in answer to His prayer in the Garden of Gethsemane.

Yes, the reason God the Father refused God the Son His request to be saved from a painful death was that He wanted to make manifest the very thing His Son had come into the world to do—to save the world. Isn't that what Jesus talked about so often during His earthly ministry—His mission, His "hour," His sacrificial death?[40] God the Father gave God the Son *exactly* what He and His Son wanted most, despite His Son's last-minute feelings of anxiety and desperation.

That's why the true model for every miracle request must always be Jesus Christ's prayer during His agony in the Garden. No matter how scared you may be; no matter how much you want to beg for a specific miracle, you must always make the decision—as Jesus did—to add to your plea: "Not my will but Your will be done."

When you say that and mean it—when you embrace this miracle paradox by being precise in your prayer yet radically open to God's providence—all the channels of grace-filled divine possibility will be *opened up to you*. Because of your willingness to give God the maximum amount of faith, hope, love, and surrender, God will find a way to answer you in a manner that fulfills your deepest desires—whether or not you immediately realize it. Sometimes, His answer will come with lightning quickness. Other times, His answer will take years or even decades to unfold, and you will recognize it only in hindsight. As Christ said to the apostles: "What I am doing you do not

[40] John 3:16; 12:23–27; 17:1; Mark 10:45.

know now, but afterward you will understand" (John 13:7, RSVCE). It all depends on what you truly want and what free choices and events in the world need to be arranged to make your prayer come true, according to the mysterious workings of providence.

But one thing you can be sure of is that God *will* answer you. That's why all the miracle promises of Christ in the Gospels were made with such clarity and certitude. It's because He *does* intend to say yes to whatever you ask; He *does* intend to give you whatever you seek; He *does* intend to open the door whenever you knock.

So, as you move forward with an open heart and mind, you should *expect* to be answered. In fact, you should expect to be surprised and even dazzled.

And as you wait, add this final petition to your miracle prayer:

Lord, help me to be as sincere, transparent, and precise as possible in expressing my needs to You as I would with my closest friends and family, but also help me to remain completely open to Your divine wisdom in fulfilling my request, knowing Your power to perceive the deepest yearnings of my soul and to grant them to me in the most unexpected ways.

Conclusion
The Miracle Prayer

Now that we've come to the end of this little book, the main point I want to leave you with is that you should have great hope in God's power and mercy and willingness to help you. Indeed, I don't believe God would have led you to this book if He didn't have something wonderful planned for you in the days, weeks, months, and years ahead.

My one fear is that we may have focused too much on the idea of seeking miracles for the purpose of staving off something bad. In other words, we think about miracles so often in a negative way because we need help to escape some kind of terrible evil, be it physical, emotional, relational, or financial. It's only human to focus on the problems we have, and yet we can't forget that the whole point of miracles is to awaken us to the larger miracles of creation and life and God's Incarnation in Jesus Christ; and the point of *those* miracles is to help us to *know, love, and serve God, so that we can be happy with Him forever in Heaven* (see CCC 1721).

The Gospel says that "the kingdom of heaven is like treasure hidden in a field. When a man found it, he hid it again, and then in his joy went and sold all he had and bought that field" (Matt. 13:44). What I've been trying to do in these pages is urge you to believe that God wants to give you a treasure—*an actual treasure*—and that you need to do everything in your power to accept and secure that treasure by embracing the miracle paradoxes we've discussed. Many of you, because of your personality type or the gifts that God has given you, might be inclined to emphasize one kind of prayer in your life or one "side" of each miracle paradox. The whole point of this book is that if—despite your natural inclinations—you implement *both* sides of *all* God's paradoxes, you will be doing the utmost to bridge the gap between the earthly and the divine and to bring down the gift of this miraculous treasure God wants to bestow upon you.

We spoke in chapter 3 about the Age of Miracles—that period in the early Church when God bestowed a super-abundance of healings and other miracles on the followers of Christ in order to help them withstand the persecutions they were enduring and evangelize the world with their Faith.

I believe that today we stand on the cusp of a *new* Age of Miracles. In the West, Christians face a different but no less dangerous form of persecution from that of their early Christian forebears. This includes the attacks on Christian values in public life, the marginalization of religious expression, and the increasing legal and social pressures against Christian teachings on issues such as marriage, sexuality, and the sanctity of life. In fact, the parallels between the early Christian period and today are too striking to ignore. Both eras are characterized by smaller, more dedicated, more purified Christian populations. Both periods witness a clear need for divine intervention to bolster faith and spread the Christian message.

And herein lies our hope—because, just as the need to evangelize amid persecution ushered in the Age of Miracles in the first centuries of Christianity, so the latest wave of persecution and faithlessness might usher in a new age of miracles in the twenty-first century. Indeed, though the Church herself is undergoing a season of internal conflict and confusion, she has recognized the need to address this desperate situation. On September 21, 2010,

Pope Benedict XVI issued the apostolic letter *Ubicumque et Semper* (Always and everywhere) to establish the Pontifical Council for Promoting the New Evangelization.

Why would we need a new evangelization? It's not because there's a new gospel. It's because the same gospel we've always had must be preached anew to a world that has largely forgotten the Christian faith. And because of this necessity, it makes sense that there might also be a new and accompanying wave of miracles.

The bottom line is that you should be excited about the prospect of praying for a miracle today. In fact, you shouldn't pray for just one; you should pray for as many as you need. You should use this time of purification to obtain the miracles God wants to give you, as well as to proclaim His greater glory so that you yourself can help spread the gospel more effectively to a world that desperately needs it.

Let me emphasize this last point because it represents a "bonus" paradox we haven't talked about at length. For, though it's a given that all prayers of supplication express the desires of our heart, their primary purpose should always be to reveal God's presence, power, and majesty to the world. In other words, when you ask God for a miracle, you should simultaneously ask Him to use your answered prayer to deepen the faith of those around you, to make them realize that *God* is responsible for the great blessing you're receiving. When you seek God's glory in your prayers, you acknowledge that your requests are not solely about fulfilling selfish desires but about spreading faith in God to everyone.

And that's the whole point of authentic spirituality, isn't it—to deepen faith in God and, consequently, help more souls to be saved so that they can share in God's happiness, here and in the next world? Putting the focus on God's glory ensures that any prayers you say are oriented in the correct way—toward accomplishing God's divine plan. This reflects not only a humble disposition but a mature faith, one more worthy and deserving of a miracle.

Indeed, the Bible is replete with evidence that this kind of prayer not only works but acts as a kind of "tractor beam" for the miraculous![41]

So, despite any apprehension you might have, keep the faith! I say to you again, if the world and all its problems are becoming too much for you to handle and you find yourself desperate and afraid, try to give all your fear,

[41] Exod. 32:11–14; Ezek. 36:22–23; 1 Kings 18:36–39; Josh. 7:8–9; Dan. 9:17–19; John 11:41–42; 17:1–5.

dread, doubt, and anxiety to the One who said, "*Be of good cheer*, for I have overcome the world" (John 16:33, RSVCE).

And if you're praying for a miracle for someone else, remember my friend Fr. Brian. When I've asked him why he has been the recipient of so many miraculous answers to prayer, he always says the same thing:

> The Holy Spirit is infinite. When He's living inside you, when He has made your body His home, and when you're comfortable with His presence, it's much easier for you to share Him with others. Indeed, the Holy Spirit doesn't want to be "hogged." He wants you to give Him as a gift to those who need Him most, over and over again.

So, if you want to help or heal others, in addition to implementing the strategies in this book, try your best to get your spiritual house in order, invite the Holy Spirt to come and live inside you, be generous in sharing His presence, go outside your comfort zone when praying, and boldly ask for the impossible as often as you can. Then watch with amazement as God begins to use *you* as an instrument for His miraculous activity in the world.

I've taken the liberty of putting all the miracle paradoxes we've discussed into one miracle prayer below. If you need a miracle, I encourage you to print out this prayer or copy or scan it onto your smartphone and read it every day—when possible, before the Blessed Sacrament. I'm telling you, something amazing is going to happen. I can't guarantee that you'll obtain the specific miracle you're requesting, but as God is my witness, you're going to receive something in answer to prayer that you didn't anticipate, something that will help you and your loved ones in a profound way.

Finally, I want to encourage you to contact me at my website, www.anthonydestefano.com, and let me know how your miracle prayer was answered. Please know that as I've completed each page of this book, I have fervently prayed that you will receive the miracle you truly want.

God bless you!

THE MIRACLE PRAYER

Most Holy Trinity—Father, Son, and Holy Spirit:

Thank You for bringing me to a point in my life where I realize that I need the kind of help only You can provide. Despite the weight of my problems, at least I am no longer living under the delusion that I am self-sufficient. I know I need a miracle right now, and I know I must come to

You to obtain it. I stand before You empty-handed, filled with faith, hope, and love, to humbly ask for the following miracle: [State your request].

Lord, I know You created the universe and the laws that govern it and that nothing You do contradicts that order. Help me to recognize Your hand in all that unfolds, whether miraculous or not, and help me to embrace the deeper truths of Your divine plan that are revealed through the paradoxes of the Christian faith.

Graciously hear my prayer, and if it be in accordance with Your holy will, grant what I seek. Yet, aware of my own limited understanding, look deep into my soul and give me what I truly desire.

Help me to benefit and grow from the tribulation You are permitting me to endure. But also grant me the courage to triumph over my anxiety and seek whatever help I need to rise above the challenges I face as I await Your miraculous intervention in my life.

Give me the patience, persistence, and perseverance I need to keep entreating Your aid, even if my request is not immediately answered. But give me the faith to make a definitive decision to believe in Your power and willingness to provide what is necessary for the good of my soul.

Help me to fulfill all my duties and take the actions necessary to overcome my problems. But even as I diligently carry out my responsibilities, help me to trust, abandon, and surrender myself entirely to Your divine will.

Help me to repent of all my past sins and die to myself, for the purpose of transforming into my best, true self—the person You created me to be—and someone worthy of receiving Your miraculous assistance.

Help me to strengthen my personal relationship with You—especially through the worthy reception of the Blessed Sacrament—and to strengthen my relationship within Your community of believers, as I ask my brothers and sisters in Christ to intercede on my behalf.

Help me to be as sincere, transparent, and precise as possible in expressing my needs as I would with my closest friends and family. But also help me to remain completely open to Your omniscient wisdom in fulfilling my request, knowing Your power to perceive the deepest yearnings of my soul, to grant them to me in the most unexpected ways, and to bring good out of even the most painful experiences.

Filled with praise and gratitude, I pray for this miracle with my words, mind, heart, and soul for Your greater honor and glory and so that your power and majesty might be revealed to the world during this time when Your holy gospel needs to be spread anew.

In making this request, I seek the intercession of all the angels and saints in Heaven, in particular St. Jude, St. Anthony, St._____ [choose one or more saints from the list in appendix 1], and especially the Blessed Virgin Mary, Mother of God, at whose request You performed Your first miracle, at Cana.

In Jesus' Holy Name, I pray.
Amen.

Appendix 1
Saints Who Can Intercede on Your Behalf

Here is a general listing of saints frequently invoked by Catholics to intercede for them in obtaining miracles as well as assisting them with various problems of life:

Impossible Causes

St. Jude Thaddeus
St. Anthony of Padua
St. Rita of Cascia
St. Philomena
St. Gregory Thaumaturgus

Specific Health Problems

Blindness and vision problems: St. Lucy
Brain and neurological problems: St. Dymphna
Cancer: St. Peregrine

Chronic pain and disabilities: St. Pio of Pietrelcina
(Padre Pio), St. Lidwina of Schiedam

Deafness and hearing problems: St. Cadoc,
St. Francis de Sales

Diabetes: St. Josemaría Escrivá

Foot conditions: St. Peter

General healing: St. Raphael the Archangel,
St. Charbel of Lebanon

General infections: St. Agrippina

General pain: St. Madron

Headaches: St. Teresa of Ávila

Heart conditions: St. John of God

Injuries: St. John Licci

Mental health issues: St. Dymphna, St. Benedict
Joseph Labre, St. Michael the Archangel

Muscle and skeletal problems: St. Alphonsus
Liguori, St. Drogo

Pediatric diseases: St. Philomena

Skin conditions: St. Anthony the Abbot,
St. Peregrine

Surgery: St. Luke the Evangelist

Toothache: St. Apollonia

Treatment of diseases: St. Raphael the Archangel

Evil Forces and Possessions

St. Michael the Archangel

Overcoming Big Sins

St. Augustine of Hippo

Overcoming Addictions

St. Maximilian Kolbe
Ven. Matt Talbot
St. Mark Ji Tianxiang

Financial Problems

St. Matthew
St. Nicholas of Myra
St. Raphael the Archangel
St. Cajetan
St. Joseph the Worker

Relationship Problems

St. Rita of Cascia
St. Valentine
St. John Macias

Finding a Husband or Wife

St. Raphael the Archangel

St. Anne

St. Joseph

St. Andrew

St. Paraskeva

St. Valentine

Marital Problems and Family Happiness

St. Joseph

St. Anne

Bl. Concepción Cabrera de Armida

Becoming Pregnant and Safe Pregnancies

St. Gerard Majella

St. Anne

St. Colette

St. Gianna Beretta Molla

St. Catherine of Sweden

St. Rita of Cascia

St. Brigid of Kildare

St. Anne

St. Elizabeth

Problems with Children

> St. Nicholas of Myra
> St. Philomena
> St. José Sánchez del Río

Converting Others to the Faith

> St. Joseph of Cupertino
> St. Thomas Aquinas

Studies and Exams

> St. Joseph of Cupertino
> St. Thomas Aquinas

Achieving Longevity

> St. Peter

Saving the Life or Soul, or Both, of a Person on the Verge of Death

> St. Joseph
> St. Rita of Cascia
> St. Faustina Kowalska

The Miraculous Medal

The Miraculous Medal, revealed to St. Catherine Labouré in 1830, has been linked to countless miracles and conversions since its introduction. It is perhaps the best-known Catholic sacramental, and wearing it is seen as a physical expression of faith, particularly when asking God for His grace through the intercession of the Blessed Virgin Mary. Catholic sacramentals are rooted in biblical examples of physical objects conveying God's grace. For instance, in the Gospels, a woman was healed by touching the hem of Jesus' garment (Luke 8:44), and in Acts, St. Paul's handkerchiefs were used to heal the sick (19:11-12). These instances show that God can use material objects as instruments of grace. It's important to clarify that the Miraculous Medal itself is in no way a source of magic or superstition or idolatry; rather, its power lies in the wearer's faith and the prayers that accompany it. The medal serves as a reminder to trust in God's mercy and grace, with Mary being a compassionate intercessor who points us toward Christ. This makes it a helpful spiritual tool for those seeking miracles or divine assistance.

Appendix 2
Inspirational Bible Verses on Fear, Trust, and Miracles

From the beginning, I've envisioned this book to be a resource you can use if you're in genuine need of a miracle. The following Bible passages have provided inspiration and hope to people in various kinds of trouble for thousands of years. So, if you're in the hospital waiting to have surgery, or if you have some huge bills to pay and don't have the money, or if someone you love is in danger and there's nothing else for you to do, I encourage you to read these passages prayerfully. Remember, this is the Word of God, and God can neither deceive nor be deceived. What He says here is the truth, and you can put your faith in Him.

Psalm 91, often called the "Psalm of Protection," has been a source of comfort and strength for countless individuals facing difficulties. Throughout history, people have turned to its verses during times of fear, illness, and danger, finding reassurance in its promises of God's refuge, deliverance, and protection.

Psalm 91 (RSVCE)

> He who dwells in the shelter of the Most High,
>> who abides in the shadow of the Almighty,
> will say to the Lord, "My refuge and my fortress;
>> my God, in whom I trust."
> For he will deliver you from the snare of the
>> fowler
>> and from the deadly pestilence;
> he will cover you with his pinions,
>> and under his wings you will find refuge;
>> his faithfulness is a shield and buckler.
> You will not fear the terror of the night,
>> nor the arrow that flies by day,
> nor the pestilence that stalks in darkness,
>> nor the destruction that wastes at noonday.
>
> A thousand may fall at your side,
>> ten thousand at your right hand;
>> but it will not come near you.

You will only look with your eyes
  and see the recompense of the wicked.

Because you have made the Lord your refuge,
  the Most High your habitation,
no evil shall befall you,
  no scourge come near your tent.

For he will give his angels charge of you
  to guard you in all your ways.
 On their hands they will bear you up,
  lest you dash your foot against a stone.
You will tread on the lion and the adder,
  the young lion and the serpent you will trample
  under foot.

Because he cleaves to me in love, I will deliver him;
  I will protect him, because he knows my name.
When he calls to me, I will answer him;
  I will be with him in trouble,
  I will rescue him and honor him.

With long life I will satisfy him,
  and show him my salvation.

Psalm 23, often referred to as "The Lord is my Shepherd," has likewise been a source of profound solace for thousands of years. This psalm's powerful imagery and assurance of God's guidance and protection have offered hope and peace to those enduring suffering, reminding them of God's unwavering presence and care in times of need.

Psalm 23 (RSVCE)

The Lord is my shepherd, I shall not want;
he makes me lie down in green pastures.
He leads me beside still waters;
he restores my soul.
He leads me in paths of righteousness
for his name's sake.

Even though I walk through the valley of the
shadow of death,
I fear no evil;
for thou art with me;
thy rod and thy staff,
they comfort me.

Thou preparest a table before me
in the presence of my enemies;

thou anointest my head with oil,
my cup overflows.
Surely goodness and mercy shall follow me
all the days of my life;
and I shall dwell in the house of the Lord
for ever.

Here are some verses from other psalms known for their power to provide strength in the face of adversity:

But you, LORD, are a shield around me, my glory, the One who lifts my head high. I call out to the LORD, and he answers me from his holy mountain. I lie down and sleep; I wake again because the Lord sustains me. I will not fear though tens of thousands assail me on every side. (Ps. 3:3–6)

Keep me safe, O God; in you I take refuge. I say to the LORD, You are my Lord, you are my only good.... LORD, my allotted portion and my cup, you have made my destiny secure. Pleasant places were measured out for me; fair to me indeed is my [eternal] inheritance. I bless the LORD who counsels me; even at night my heart exhorts me. I keep the LORD always before me; with him at my right hand, I shall never be shaken. (Ps. 16:1–2, 5–8, NABRE)

The LORD is my light and my salvation; whom should I fear? The Lord is my life's refuge; of whom should I be afraid? When evildoers come at me to devour my flesh, these my enemies and foes themselves stumble and fall. Though an army encamp against me, my heart does not fear; though war be waged against me, even then do I trust. (Ps. 27:1–3, NABRE)

I waited patiently for the LORD; he inclined to me and heard my cry. He drew me up from the desolate pit, out of the miry bog, and set my feet upon a rock, making my steps secure. He put a new song in my mouth, a song of praise to our God. Many will see and fear and put their trust in the LORD. (Ps. 40:1–3, RSVCE)

God is our refuge and strength, a very present help in trouble. Therefore we will not fear, though the earth gives way and the mountains fall into the heart of the sea. (Ps. 46:1–2)

Be still and know that I am God; I will be exalted among the nations, I will be exalted in the earth. (Ps. 46:10)

As for me, I call to God, and the LORD saves me. Evening, morning and noon, I cry out in distress, and he hears my voice. (Ps. 55:16–17)

I sought the LORD, and he answered me; he delivered me from all my fears. Those who look to him are radiant; their faces are never covered with shame. This poor man called, and the LORD heard him; he saved him out of all his troubles. The angel of the Lord encamps around those who fear him, and he delivers them. (Ps. 34:4–7)

I lift up my eyes to the mountains—where does my help come? My help comes from the LORD, the Maker of heaven and earth. He will not let your foot slip; he who watches over you will not slumber. (Ps. 121:1–3)

When I called, you answered me; you greatly emboldened me.... Though I walk in the midst of trouble, you preserve my life. You stretch out your hand against the anger of my foes; with your right hand you save me. (Ps. 138:3, 7)

God is our refuge and strength, an ever-present help in trouble. Therefore we will not fear, though the earth give way and the mountains fall into the heart of the sea, though its waters roar and foam and the mountains quake with their surging. (Ps. 46:1–3)

Here are some Bible verses particularly suited for those going through difficult times and in need of miraculous answers to prayer:

I am the LORD, your healer. (Exod. 15:26, RSVCE)

Have I not commanded you? Be strong and courageous. Do not be afraid; do not be discouraged, for the LORD your God will be with you wherever you go. (Josh. 1:9)

Ask and it will be given to you; seek and you will find; knock and the door will be opened to you. For everyone who asks receives; the one who seeks finds; and to the one who knocks, the door will be opened." (Matt. 7:7–8)

Therefore I tell you, do not worry about your life, what you will eat or drink; or about your body, what you will wear. Is not life more than food, and the body more than clothes?... Therefore do not worry about tomorrow, for tomorrow will worry about itself. Each day has enough trouble of its own. (Matt. 6:25, 34)

For truly, I say to you, if you have faith as a grain of mustard seed, you will say to this mountain, "Move from hence to yonder place," and it will move; and nothing will be impossible to you. (Matt. 17:20, RSVCE)

Truly I tell you, if you have faith and do not doubt ... you can say to this mountain, "Go, throw yourself into the sea," and it will be done. If you believe, you will receive whatever you ask for in prayer. (Matt. 21:21–22)

Everything is possible for one who believes. (Mark 9:23)

Therefore I tell you, whatever you ask for in prayer, believe that you have received it, and it will be yours. (Mark 11:24)

Taking her by the hand, he said to her, "Talitha cumi"; which means, "Little girl, I say to you, arise." And immediately the girl got up and walked; for she was twelve years old. And immediately they were overcome with amazement. (Mark 5:41–42)

What is impossible with men is possible with God. (Luke 18:27)

On the third day a wedding took place at Cana in Galilee. Jesus' mother was there, and Jesus and his disciples had also been invited to the wedding. When the wine was gone, Jesus' mother said to him, "They have no more wine." "Woman, why do you involve me?" Jesus replied. "My hour has not yet come." His mother said to the servants, "Do whatever he tells you." Nearby stood six stone water jars, the kind used by the Jews for ceremonial washing, each holding from twenty to thirty gallons. Jesus said to the servants, "Fill the jars with water"; so they filled them to the brim. Then he told them, "Now draw some out and take it to the master of the banquet." They did so, and the master of the banquet tasted the water that had been turned into wine. He did not realize where it had come from, though the servants who had drawn the water knew. Then he called the bridegroom aside and said, "Everyone brings out the choice wine first and then the cheaper wine after the guests have had too much to drink; but you have saved the best till now." What Jesus did here in Cana of Galilee was the first of the signs through which he revealed his glory; and his disciples believed in him. (John 2:1–11)

I am the living bread which came down from heaven; if any one eats of this bread, he will live for ever; and the bread which I shall give for the life of the world is my flesh. (John 6:51, RSVCE)

Jesus said to her, "Your brother will rise again." Martha answered, "I know he will rise again in the resurrection at the last day. Jesus said to her, "I am the resurrection and the life. The one who believes in me will live, even though they die; and whoever lives by believing in me will never die." (John 11:23–26)

Whatever you ask in my name, I will do it, that the Father may be glorified in the Son; if you ask anything in my name, I will do it. (John 14:13–14, RSVCE)

Peace I leave with you; my peace I give you. I do not give to you as the world gives. Do not let your hearts be troubled and do not be afraid. (John 14:27)

If you remain in me and my words remain in you, ask whatever you wish, and it will be done for you. (John 15:7)

I have told you these things, so that in me you may have peace. In this world, you will have trouble. But take heart! I have overcome the world." (John 16:33)

And we know that in all things God works for the good of those who love him, who have been called according to his purpose. (Rom. 8:28)

For I am convinced that neither death nor life, neither angels nor demons, neither the present nor the future, nor any powers, neither height nor depth, nor anything else in all creation, will be able to separate us from the love of God that is in Christ Jesus our Lord. (Rom. 8:38–39)

The Spirit you received does not make you slaves, so that you live in fear again; rather, the Spirit you received brought about your adoption to sonship. And by him we cry, "*Abba*, Father." (Rom. 8:15)

For we live by faith, not by sight. (2 Cor. 5:7)

Do not be anxious about anything, but in every situation, by prayer and petition, with thanksgiving, present your requests to God. And the peace of God, which transcends all understanding, will guard your hearts and your minds in Christ Jesus. (Phil. 4:6–7)

I can do all this through him who gives me strength. (Phil. 4:13)

For the Spirit God gave us does not make us timid, but gives us power, love, and self-discipline. (2 Tim. 1:7)

Now faith is confidence in what we hope for and assurance about what we do not see. (Heb. 11:1)

So we say with confidence, "The Lord is my helper; I will not be afraid. What can mere mortals do to me?" (Heb. 13:6)

Consider it pure joy, my brothers and sisters, whenever you face trials of many kinds, because you know that the testing of your faith produces perseverance. Let perseverance finish its work so that you may be mature and complete, not lacking anything. (James 1:2–4)

Cast all your anxiety on him because he cares for you. (1 Pet. 5:7)

He will wipe away every tear from their eyes, and death shall be no more, neither shall there be mourning nor crying nor pain any more, for the former things have passed away. And he who sat upon the throne said, "Behold, I make all things new." (Rev. 21:4–5)

Acknowledgments

Contrary to popular belief, writing is rarely a solitary endeavor. Every book is the result of a collaborative effort, and I am deeply grateful to the many people who played a role in bringing this work to life.

First and foremost, I extend my sincere thanks to the incredible team at Sophia Institute Press, including its president, Charlie McKinney, its vice president, Tom Allen, and every member of the Sophia staff who contributed to this project: Sarah Lemieux, Molly Russo, Sheila Perry, Anna Maria Dube, Molly Rublee, Ryan Staples, and Caleb Selecter. I am especially indebted to my brilliant editors, Heidi Hess Saxton and Nora Malone, for their keen insights and careful attention to detail.

I also wish to express my gratitude to my dear friend and former editor at Penguin Random House, Michelle

Rapkin—the very first person to read and critique this book. Her wisdom and experience were invaluable.

A special thanks goes to Fr. Matthew S. Ernest, Fr. Mark Vaillancourt, Msgr. Joseph P. LaMorte, and my brother Fr. Salvatore DeStefano of the Archdiocese of New York for their assistance in obtaining the imprimatur for this book. I am also grateful to Fr. Peter M. J. Stravinskas for his scholarly guidance on the subject of miracles and to Fr. Brian, "the "Miracle Priest," for his profound insights and inspiring stories.

Throughout the writing and final editing of this book, I had the great fortune of working in the home of my sister-in-law, Shiloah Lisech, and her husband, Andrew. Their warm hospitality and the dedicated writing space they provided were a true gift, helping me to bring this book to completion.

I would be remiss if I did not acknowledge my dear friend and late literary manager, Peter Miller. This was among the last books he championed for me, and I miss his wisdom and steadfast support every day.

Finally, and most importantly, I thank my beloved wife, Jordan, whose unwavering encouragement sustained me through every stage of this process—especially during the most difficult moments. Her love and support mean everything to me.

About the Author

Anthony DeStefano is the bestselling author of many Christian books for adults and children. Born in Brooklyn and raised in New York City, he now lives in New Jersey with his wife, Jordan.

Sophia Institute

Sophia Institute is a nonprofit institution that seeks to nurture the spiritual, moral, and cultural life of souls and to spread the gospel of Christ in conformity with the authentic teachings of the Roman Catholic Church.

Sophia Institute Press fulfills this mission by offering translations, reprints, and new publications that afford readers a rich source of the enduring wisdom of mankind.

Sophia Institute also operates the popular online resource CatholicExchange.com. *Catholic Exchange* provides world news from a Catholic perspective as well as daily devotionals and articles that will help readers to grow in holiness and live a life consistent with the teachings of the Church.

In 2013, Sophia Institute launched Sophia Institute for Teachers to renew and rebuild Catholic culture through service to Catholic education. With the goal of nurturing the spiritual, moral, and cultural life of souls, and an abiding respect for the role and work of teachers, we strive to provide materials and programs that are at once enlightening to the mind and ennobling to the heart; faithful and complete, as well as useful and practical.

Sophia Institute gratefully recognizes the Solidarity Association for preserving and encouraging the growth of our apostolate over the course of many years. Without their generous and timely support, this book would not be in your hands.

www.SophiaInstitute.com
www.CatholicExchange.com
www.SophiaInstituteforTeachers.org

Sophia Institute Press® is a registered trademark of Sophia Institute. Sophia Institute is a tax-exempt institution as defined by the Internal Revenue Code, Section 501(c)(3). Tax ID 22-2548708.